И

As a Jewish anti-Zionist, I am on the same side with Alex McDonald. Even so, I do not agree 100% with everything in this guide. However, Alex makes me think about how, where, and why I disagree. And this is Alex's point -- that we need to avoid our own knee-jerk reactions and think things through, both for ourselves and with those on the other side of this contentious issue. For anti-racists, this is a valuable resource for practicing how (rather than what) to think and how to get the other side to think.

Alan Wagman

From 1949 to 1961 I lived in Saudi Arabia and listened to the eyewitness accounts of Palestinians who were recent victims of the Nakba. I was also aboard the USS Liberty when the Israeli military attacked the ship on June 8, 1967. A lifetime of research into both catastrophes has enabled me to take part in fact-based discussions of both. Alex McDonald has provided a valuable service to those unfamiliar with the specifics of the Israel/Palestine issues who want to engage in a conversation based on facts and not hyperbole. I highly recommend his work.

Joe Meadors

WHEN THEY
SPEAK ISRAEL

WHEN THEY SPEAK ISRAEL

*A Guide to Clarity in
Conversations about Israel*

ALEX MCDONALD

Great Tree Publishing, LLC
Houston, Texas

Published by Great Tree Publishing, LLC, Houston, TX
GreatTreePublishing.com
Copyright © 2021 Alex McDonald
All rights reserved.
Edited by Allan Edmands

LCCN: 2021900297
ISBN: 978-1-954221-01-7
ISBN: 978-1-954221-02-4 (ebook)

*To all who stand for human rights
and treating others as they want to be treated*

The single biggest problem in
communication is the illusion
that it has taken place.

—George Bernard Shaw

Contents

Preface and Acknowledgments

This guide came out of my feeling frustrated. I could not communicate effectively with people I care deeply for: my family and friends. I could not communicate with them concerning a topic I care deeply about: the values of equality and justice.

I want to first thank those family members and friends who were willing to tell me that they wanted to end conversations or stop reading my emails and writings on Israel/Palestine. I really appreciate those who were kind enough to tell me *why* they objected to what I was saying and writing. Without their kindness and willingness to tell me their concerns, I would not have been able to progress on my own journey. These concerns forced me to clarify distinctions for myself and explore additional positions of others.

I especially want to thank a number of people who have been extremely generous with their time and recommendations as I have developed my writings. To protect them from the abuse and retribution that is all too commonly directed toward people who expose information on Israel/Palestine, I will not name them here. Nonetheless, I would like to share my admiration and gratitude for their love for all people and for human rights generally; they are truly inspiring. I am honored to walk for peace and justice with them—and with you—as we work together to end all oppression.

Peace to all.

Introduction

Israel/Palestine:
The Difficult but Necessary Conversation

If we Americans want peace in the Middle East, if we want US policies to reflect our values of freedom, equality, and human rights, then we need to have conversations on the Israel/Palestine issue. We need to talk about Israel/Palestine because we are the major outside supporter of the current situation.

I use the term *Israel/Palestine* to describe a land area and its state(s). The term *Israel* seems incomplete and inaccurate as a descriptor because the state of Israel has never defined its borders. In particular, Israel claims and controls land that the international community calls "the occupied Palestinian territories." *Palestine* also seems incomplete and confusing because although most of the countries of the world recognize the state of Palestine, they recognize borders different from those of historic Palestine under the British Mandate (1923–1948). The term *Israel/Palestine* therefore seems most appropriate to define a piece of land for which there is currently no universally accepted name.

Conversations about Israel/Palestine can be difficult, especially for people who do not engage in them regularly. If you are not careful, such conversations can quickly turn into confrontation—or worse, animosity. I wrote this guide to help you have successful Israel/Palestine conversations—conversations that are thoughtful and introspective rather than accusatory and argumentative. In a thoughtful and introspective conversation, both parties can learn and connect with each other. Remain curious and focused on learning, and the conversations will get easier.

Perhaps you believe that a successful conversation is one where you convince a person to accept your position. That's not the objective of this guide. Instead, my goal is to make you feel more comfortable in having these conversations and to highlight for you and your conversation partner the logical flaws in the messaging you may often hear concerning the Israel/Palestine situation.

Convincing someone requires a lot of knowledge about the subject. The quoted history of the state of Israel that we get in American schools and through our media has been peppered with misleading information, and separating truth from mythology can be difficult. Many people don't realize that they have been taught falsehoods. The purpose of this guide is not to correct the mythology; rather, it is to equip you in identifying logical flaws in the mythology and messaging. To distinguish truth from mythology, check out my other book *How I Learned to Speak Israel*; it provides detailed historical accounts and information on the current situation which will be helpful to you on your journey.

This guide is a stepping stone on your path to feeling comfortable talking about Israel/Palestine, to understanding the foundational values that cause division on this subject. In this guide I will help you better understand your own position and articulate it. Skill and confidence will take practice, and this guide provides basic tools to help you practice.

When you engage in an Israel/Palestine conversation with others, I want you to meet two objectives: The first is to develop a relationship with the other person that you can maintain and, hopefully, improve over time. The second is to better understand both your own perspective and the other person's. Those two objectives are important because they enable you to go back and resume conversations, each time developing knowledge and confidence.

The best way to be heard and understood is often to let your conversation partner first feel heard and understood. Even if they want you to hear only their perspective, let them; you can benefit greatly by learning what they believe. Use them as your teacher, and learn by asking clarifying questions.

Telling your conversation partner that their "facts" are false will not help you meet your two objectives. Instead, take note of what your partner believes and hold them to it. Your job is to hold them to their "truths" by forcing them to be consistent in their beliefs and story. Let their own narrative highlight any inherent discrepancies. For example, if they say that the wall in the West Bank is there to protect Jews from the Palestinians, then ask why there are more than one million Palestinians on the Israeli side of the wall. Don't tell them they are wrong about Israel being defensive; rather, ask them to explain how Israel was defensive when it was the first to attack and then when it captured so much land that it more than doubled its area in the 1967 Six-Day War.

Different Facts, Beliefs, and Narratives

When you and your conversation partner hold different facts, beliefs, and narratives, conversations are difficult. Some of these "facts" can be basic, such as what a map of Israel looks like. Some people include East Jerusalem and the West Bank as part of Israel, whereas others do not. Some include the Golan Heights and Shebaa Farms, while others do not. Minimize assumptions. Ask for specifics. Get clarification.

Zionists believe that Jews have a right to a state in historic Palestine. Some of these supporters of the state of Israel believe the Bible[1] is the Jews' deed to the land. Others believe Jews deserve the land because of historic anti-Semitism, the Holocaust, the 1917 Balfour Declaration,

---

1   *Bible* refers to Scripture shared by the Abrahamic faiths.

or the United Nations vote to partition Palestine in 1947. Many Jewish Zionists believe that a Jewish state is needed for their safety, that the elimination of a Jewish state would be tantamount to genocide. Zionists often believe that Israel is always on the defensive, dealing with attacks from neighboring countries and from terrorists within. Many American Zionists, Christian and Jewish, believe that the United States should be a strong supporter of its ally Israel for the reasons previously stated. They also want the US to support Israel because Israel represents Judeo-Christian/Western values and ethics in the Middle East. This guide refers to this Zionist view as the Israeli perspective or narrative.

I wrote this guide for anti-Zionists, specifically people who oppose policies of a state that give preferential rights to one ethnic group at the expense of the human rights of another ethnic group. We oppose all forms of racism and believe that the Universal Declaration of Human Rights needs to be honored. We believe that all people should have self-determination—particularly within a country that claims to be a democracy. We believe that everyone should have equal rights, regardless of their ethnicity or religion. Anti-Zionists believe that Zionists, represented by the state of Israel, are the aggressors, as evidenced by more than fifty years of occupation and seventy years of violations of human rights and international law. American anti-Zionists believe that the United States should not fund the Israeli military's oppressive occupation of Palestinians. Many anti-

Zionists support boycotting Israeli products as well as academic and cultural events, just as the Anti-Apartheid Movement did as a form of peaceful protest during the last half of the twentieth century against South Africa.

When They Speak Israel may also be helpful to people who consider themselves balanced or slightly Zionist-leaning. They may want to understand why someone would be anti-Zionist. They may want to read what the "other side" believes, what the anti-Zionist strategy is. Who knows? Once they read it, they may see a connection between Zionism and racism and think: "You know, anti-racism isn't a bad idea!"

Differences in Language

Zionists and anti-Zionists don't always realize we speak different languages, and that also makes conversations about Israel/Palestine difficult. Although we both sound like we are speaking English, we assign different meanings to words, including *democracy*, *security*, *defensive*, *peace*, and *terrorist*. Zionists tend to define *democracy* as the ability of only citizens to elect leaders, where ethnicity or religion can determine citizenship. For anti-Zionists, on the other hand, *democracy* requires equality, and with it the ability of the governed to elect those who rule over them. *Security* for Zionists means protection of a system that gives one ethnic group control over the land and the other population; for anti-Zionists, *security* means protection from oppression and from violation of human rights. *Peace* means control to Zionists, whereas it requires equality and justice to anti-Zionists.

If the foregoing terms and their definitions are confusing, don't worry; the pro-Israel messaging is designed to be confusing. The issue is relatively simple, however; the issue is discrimination and human rights violation. But because those in power don't want us to see the problem as simple, they make it sound complicated and confusing. The more we unpack pro-Israel messaging, the more convoluted and confusing the Zionist arguments. It takes confusion to convince people that standing for equality is anti-Semitic. It takes confusion and fear to convince people that the only way to be safe is to oppress others and take land by force from them. This guide is designed to help you and your conversation partner see through the fog.

Be alert to definition differences because they can easily cause misunderstanding and even animosity. If you and your conversation partner have different understandings of words, then you are not communicating. I recommend you share your definition of words and ask them to define their words as well.

The following are some definitions of words and terms I use in this guide. These definitions are neither better nor more accurate than definitions found elsewhere; they are merely explanations for what I mean when I use these terms in this guide. These terms have multiple definitions, and if we don't specify which definition we are using, then we are likely miscommunicating.

anti-Zionist.

Or **anti-Zionism.** An anti-Zionist is someone who opposes all racism and therefore opposes a state where one ethnic group (in this case, Jews) has privilege over another (Palestinians). Although there are people who oppose Israel as a Jewish state because they are anti-Jewish, such people are not included in this guide's definition of *anti-Zionist.*

Some people conflate anti-Zionism with anti-Semitism. However, anti-Zionists, unlike anti-Semites, want Jews to be safe. We anti-Zionists stand for peace and equality, and we believe that Israel is fueling anti-Jewish sentiment by perpetrating violations of human rights in the name of Jews.

ethnic.

Here is the definition according to Merriam-Webster:[1]

of or relating to large groups of people classed according to common racial, national, tribal, religious, linguistic, or cultural origin or background.

Notice that this definition is broad, that ethnic discrimination significantly overlaps with racial discrimination. This guide considers ethnic discrimination a form of racism. See also *race* and *racism*.

Israel.

The term *Israel* usually refers to the country represented in the United Nations. *Israel* also refers to the country's government.

This guide also uses the term *Israel* to refer to a language, which has a particular way of framing and describing the Israel/Palestine situation. See also *Israelspeak*.

Israelspeak.

An individual expression (statement or question) or series of expressions—essentially a messaging—in the Israel language, which you need to comprehend and respond to.

Israeli.

A citizen of the state of Israel. Citizens include Jews and non-Jews. For example, approximately 20 percent of Israelis are Palestinian Israelis.

Jew.

Or *Jewish.* Someone of Jewish descent. As described in this guide, a Jew is either (a) a person of Jewish ethnicity or (b) an adherent of Judaism—or both. Note that there are also ethnic Jews of different

Jewish ethnicities: Sephardic, Ashkenazi, Mizrahi, and Beta Israel (Ethiopian) Jews.

Jewish state.

A state where Jews have privileges over non-Jews. The Jewish state grants rights to Jews worldwide at the expense of Palestinian human rights.

Palestinian.

A descendant of someone who lived in Palestine prior to 1948 other than anyone who does not self-identify as Palestinian; Palestinians are overwhelmingly Arab. (For example, many Ashkenazi Jews immigrated to Palestine in the early twentieth century and had Palestinian passports; their children had Palestinian birth certificates. Nonetheless, many do not consider themselves Palestinian today. There are, however, Palestinian Jews whose families have lived in Palestine for centuries and who consider themselves both Jewish and Palestinian.)

Palestinians have different legal statuses: They might be citizens of Israel, residents of Jerusalem, subjects under Israeli occupation in the West Bank or Gaza, registered refugees in refugee camps in the occupied territories or in other countries, or residents of the diaspora. Note that there are minority Arab groups—namely, the Druze and Bedouin—who usually do not consider themselves Palestinian but are included in this definition because they are discriminated against for not being Jewish.

race.

Merriam-Webster has different definitions of *race*, including the following:[2]

> a family, tribe, people, or nation belonging to the same stock.

> a class or kind of people unified by shared interests, habits, or characteristics.

> a category of humankind that shares certain distinctive physical traits.

These Merriam-Webster definitions are extremely broad. See *racism* for clarification.

racism.

Or *racist.* Racism is the preferential treatment of one ethnic group over another. This definition is based on the International Convention on the Elimination of All Forms of Racial Discrimination (ICERD), which includes the following definition of *racial discrimination*:

> any distinction, exclusion, restriction or preference based on race, colour, descent, or national or ethnic origin which has the purpose or effect of nullifying or impairing the recognition, enjoyment or exercise, on an equal footing, of human rights and

fundamental freedoms in the political, economic, social, cultural or any other field of public life.3

Since anti-racism is this guide's primary theme, I want you to be clear about my definition of *racism*. I also want you to understand why I chose that definition.

We are fighting racism based not only on how race is defined according to physically visible features (see the first definition of *race*). Whites discriminating against Blacks is clearly an example of racism, and it is a problem. But racism is also exemplified by English discriminating against Poles and by Aryans discriminating against Jews and Romanis. Therefore, when we are fighting racism, we want a broad definition that is not limited to just physical features. A superior and more inclusive definition is based on descent, family, or tribe. The problem we are fighting is not that person A is discriminating against person B because B doesn't look like A; the problem is that A is discriminating against B because B is not like A, because B comes from a different background. See also *ethnic*.

Zionist.

Or **Zionism.** A Zionist is someone who chooses to believe that Jews have the right to a state where Jews have preferential, if not exclusive, rights in, or to, historic Palestine. The *Zionist position* is also referred to in this guide as the *Israeli position*. Zionists are typically Jewish or Christian, although clearly not all Jews nor all Christians are Zionists. And although a majority of Israelis are Zionists, not all Israelis—especially not the Palestinian Israelis—are Zionists.

There are some people who call themselves cultural Zionists, who want Jewish culture to be preserved in Israel yet nonetheless want all people to have equal rights. Such people are not included in this guide's definition of *Zionist*, because they oppose any preferential treatment of people based on their ethnicity or religion at the expense of others.

Some people conflate Zionism with the support of Jews. However, many Christian Zionists support Israel not so that Jews would be safe but because they want Jews to reside in Israel and there (according to Scripture) face the horrors of the Rapture in preparation for the Second Coming of Jesus Christ; they want Jews to convert to Christianity. See also *anti-Zionist*.

Why do I spend so much time and energy on defining these terms? Because both Israel/Palestine and racism are very controversial subjects. The more we can be clear up front, the less we will accidentally cause problems later. These definitions will help you better understand this guide and will provide a foundation for communicating more clearly with your conversation partner.

Here is another reason for being clear about these definitions: People who have not deeply studied Israel/ Palestine or racism may get uncomfortable when you start talking about the two being connected.

For example, this guide designates Israel as a racist country. Why is that? That designation is inescapable, considering the definition of *racism* provided in this section. The state of Israel provides preferential treatment of one ethnic group over another. In fact, not only does it give preferential treatment to one ethnicity (Jews), it does so at the expense of another ethnic group's internationally recognized human rights (Palestinians).

The assertion that Israel is a racist country can be very uncomfortable for many who consider Israel to be the sole state in the Middle East that reflects Judeo-Christian values. It may also be uncomfortable for those who believe that Israel is a democracy. The assertion may be an annoying criticism to people who consider Arabs or Muslims to be inferior or evil. And finally, the criticism of Israel as a racist state can be interpreted as an affront to people who believe that Israel is the only safe place for Jews in the world.

But note that whatever your conversation partner's beliefs may be, those beliefs do not change whether or not Israel practices racist policies. For example, that someone may choose to believe that God gave land to a particular ethnic group or that Israel is a safe place for Jews does not eliminate the fact that the state of Israel practices racist policies.

If you are reading this guide as someone who has studied Israel/Palestine and who understands the realities of the Israeli occupation and blockade, then you know of Israel's racism. If you have studied the Nakba (النكبة, *al-Nakbah*, "the Catastrophe") and know of Israel's seventy-plus-year denial of the Right of Return to Palestinians while allowing Jewish and non-Jewish Russians to immigrate, then you know of these racist policies. If you know of the July 19, 2018, "Basic Law: Israel as the Nation-State of the Jewish People," then you know that Israel claims to represent, and to be there for, Jews from around the world in preference to even its own non-Jewish citizens. Israeli Prime Minister Benjamin Netanyahu expressed it clearly in 2019: "Israel is the nation state of the Jewish people—and only it."[4]

Unfortunately, Americans—and especially American Jews—have been shielded from the truth. They have been fed messaging (Israelspeak) that encourages them to support Israel and to feel attached to Israel as if the state were a representation of the Jewish people. It's therefore understandable that Israel supporters become uncomfortable or even angry when they are faced with the reality that they are supporting racism.

As you communicate with your conversation partner, you need to be sensitive to where your partner is on their journey. Sadly, there are those who are conscious of Israel's racism yet support the state nonetheless. Some even go further and aggressively try to label you and other anti-Zionists as anti-Semitic or unreasonable. There is little hope for a productive conversation with anyone who consciously supports any form of racism. Spend your time with people who oppose all racism.

My belief and experience are that most Zionists are good people. They have supported Israel because they have thought it was the right position to take, whether to protect Jews or to support religious beliefs they have been taught. Most of those people do not realize that by supporting the state of Israel, they would be supporting racism and human rights violations.

When they become aware of their support for racism, they often go through the five stages of grief: denial, anger, bargaining, depression, and finally acceptance. As with anyone going through stages of grief, this can be a short process, or it can take decades.

During your conversations, first determine if your partner knows that their position supports racism. Then be aware of where your conversation partner is in the five stages of grief. This guide includes a number of queries for you to offer to your conversation partner; the one(s) that you choose may depend on your partner's stage of grief. Have empathy for where they are in the process, but remain firm about standing against all racism, including Israel's.

Ethnicity and racism are especially complicated in Israel because of its different levels of racism. On a major level, Jews are privileged over Palestinians. For example, Jews from across the world can easily get Israeli citizenship, but even Palestinians who have always lived in Jerusalem have a much more difficult time—if they can get citizenship at all. Another level of racism in Israel is among the Jews themselves. Ashkenazi Jews are typically in leadership roles, whereas Mizrahi and Sephardic Jews with African, Asian, Southern European, or Middle Eastern ancestry do not always have the same opportunities as the Ashkenazim. This guide focuses on the most egregious racism: the Israeli government's Jewish-versus-Palestinian racism.

Getting Clarity with All These Challenges

As you engage in conversations, your job is to listen for contradictions and illogical concepts. Listen deeply for your partners' facts, beliefs, and narratives, including what is not stated. What are the issues that are most important to them? Are they concerned about safety, acceptance in their community, integrity, security in their job, or something else?

Also listen to determine if they actually believe what they are promoting. At a business breakfast, I was talking to a Jewish acquaintance, and the topic of Israel came up. I asked him if he supported Israel. He replied, "Of course, I support Israel. You know I'm Jewish, don't you?" I felt confused because his response implied that all Jews support Israel. To clarify, I asked, "Do you believe all Jews support Israel?" He immediately turned and started talking to someone else. He apparently did not want to answer my question, which led me to believe that he knew that not all Jews support Israel. Insist on integrity by all parties in your discussions. Integrity is a foundation for meaningful relationships and productive discussions.

One of the best ways to understand your conversation partner's perspective while meeting our two objectives is to ask clarifying questions. This will bring out the facts, beliefs, narratives, and vocabulary differences that cause confusion or disagreement.

Zionists have historically asked such questions as: "Do you think a Jewish state has the right to exist?" and "Doesn't Israel have the right to defend itself?" These questions masquerade as simple yes/no questions but are actually traps. The questions are worded to encourage yes answers—answers that ultimately lead to an endorsement of racism, of a country oppressing its indigenous people. This guide provides you with questions to help you understand your conversation partner's positions—to find out how they prioritize issues and where they stand on racism.

This Guide's Format

This guide lists eighteen Israel language expressions (questions or statements). Following each of these expressions, I include similar or related expressions for reference. Then come some basic facts on the subject, facts that provide some background information. I have included some sources for validating some of these facts. Unless you know the facts extremely well, it is easy to get diverted into rabbit holes, so it is best to work only with facts that you and your conversation partner can agree on.

Facts are helpful, but, as I mentioned earlier, I want you focused less on the facts and more on the illogical nature of the Zionist narratives. Some of these facts are included in follow-up questions to your conversation partner, questions that I call queries, but again, try to use the queries that include facts with which your partner is familiar. If you want to get a strong background on the facts, please read my book *How I Learned to Speak Israel*.

I then unpack the Israel language expressions, identifying hidden messaging. I highlight the unspoken narrative, especially the parts of that narrative that are false or misleading. For example, "Doesn't Israel have the right to defend itself?" implies a narrative of a state needing to protect itself from outside enemies. However, Israel's primary "enemies" are its indigenous population, the people whom Israel oppresses and whose crime is wanting to defend themselves from the state's oppression. Once unspoken narratives become conscious, we can more objectively evaluate them.

I focus on unspoken narratives because they are the most powerful. Unspoken narratives are what we tell ourselves subconsciously. As human beings, we are most strongly convinced by the messages we create—even if we create them subconsciously. Subconscious, unspoken narratives are the most dangerous because we are not aware of them. We don't just have them; they have us. My goal is to make these unspoken narratives visible so that you and your conversation partner can evaluate them consciously.

Once the language has been unpacked, I highlight the expression's core issue. This is a succinct statement or proposition that refutes the propaganda that the expression is promoting. We can directly address only what we can name, and this subsection identifies what we need to name so that we can move toward action.

Conversations about Israel/Palestine are like an obstacle course: There are many traps and problematic paths. The next subsection provides a recommended approach, a map so that you can avoid detours and rabbit holes.

Finally, this guide provides tips on how to answer Israel expressions and leaves you with a list of queries. These queries are your tools to engage your conversation partner so that you can better understand their facts, beliefs, and logic.

Use the queries to meet our two objectives: to build the relationship and to get clarification. Most of the queries are open-ended and help to provide greater insight into your conversation partner's thinking. The yes/no queries in this guide are not trick questions; rather, they lead to direct, fundamental issues. They are intended to steer the conversation from Israelspeak to English.

You may want to invite your conversation partner to sit with a query in silence, giving you both some time to think about it; this can be for a few minutes or a few days. Taking a time-out is especially useful when the discussion is becoming emotional for either your partner or you. Instead of reacting, breathe and take the time to identify the unspoken narratives and subconscious beliefs so that you can address them consciously.

As you get answers from your conversation partner, try to understand the logic of their narrative. Who knows, they might be right! However, if their narrative docs not add up, the two of you can figure out how to resolve it together. Your partner may not have thought through the implications of their "facts" and beliefs (we often don't think about our assumptions until we are questioned or challenged). Trying to understand their thought process from genuine curiosity and with a heart focused on learning rather than preaching will develop the conversation, each of your thoughts on the subject, and your relationship.

Do not lose sight of the basic values of freedom, equality, and human rights. Be alert to any rationalization that deviates from these values, especially as part of an unspoken narrative. Such a deviation is a slippery slope. At first, we might accept discriminating against someone out of fear, in order to protect ourselves from "them," and before we know it, we are ethnically cleansing the land. That slippery slope is an integral part of Israel's history; that is part of the Zionist narrative and the Israel language.

How to Use This Guide

This guide contains many queries, too many for you to memorize. Instead, read through each Israel expression and observe how this guide unpacks it to identify the unspoken assumptions and narratives. As you develop this unpacking skill, you will become stronger and faster at coming up with your own queries. Give yourself time; even after years of my doing this, it can still take me multiple days to identify that a statement or question is Israelspeak and then unpack it.

As you face these Israel statements and questions, use the guide to help you respond. Since you will likely not have the guide with you when you are in a conversation, take notes of your meeting. If you are not sure how to answer a question, then tell your conversation partner that their question sounds important and you would like to think about it and get back with them. If you do a good job maintaining the relationship, you can go back and ask for clarification. In the meantime, you can get ideas from the guide.

Similarly, you may find yourself in an email conversation. Before jumping on the reply button, step back, sit with your conversation partner's question or statement, and look up alternative responses in this guide. Pay attention to which of your questions your partner does not answer. Often people try to avoid the core issues because they are hard to face. You may want to follow up; but do so carefully and empathetically.

Just as I am recommending that you respond with clarification queries, your conversation partner may do the same. Step back and ask yourself whether their question is a clarification question or a diversion. Beware of diversions and keep focused. The issues are racism and human rights violations and how you need to oppose rather than rationalize them.

I have divided the eighteen Israel expressions among six chapters, each chapter a "group":
   Group 1. Attacking you
   Group 2. Pressuring acceptance of a Jewish state
   Group 3. Justifying Israeli actions

Group 4. Demonizing or criticizing Palestinian actions

Group 5. Describing an alternative reality

Group 6. Claiming that Israel is like the United States

This grouping should help you understand both (a) what your partner's statement or question is really about and (b) how to more easily find it in this guide. For each of these groups, you will be more comfortable and build your self-confidence if you understand some of its basic points. Be aware that some of the Israel language statements and questions are tricky; they can cross categories. For example, if your conversation partner says, "Demanding Palestinians' Right of Return is a ploy to end the Jewish state" (expression number 11 in Group 4), that statement could mean or imply one or more of the following:

- "You are anti-Semitic because you oppose a Jewish state" (covered in Group 1 and in Group 2).

- "Israel needs to defend itself by denying the Palestinians' Right of Return" (covered in Group 3).

- "Palestinians are trying to end a Jewish state by demanding the Right of Return" (covered in Group 4, the current location of the conversation partner's statement).

Don't bother asking your partner which of the three meanings they intended, because they will likely tell you all three. Just be aware that the multiple meanings exist, and be ready to switch from one group to the next. Also, since I list each of the eighteen Israel expressions only once in this guide, you may have to search in more than one group before you find the particular statement or question you're looking for.

If you want to remember one single query, which could both keep you focused on the core issue and elicit clarity from your conversation partner, I recommend that you memorize a couple of questions that Palestinian American author and political analyst Yousef Munayyer has asked. Munayyer, who was leader of the US Campaign to End the Israeli Occupation, posed these queries to pro-Israel-minded listeners in the audience at a debate he had in 2015 with a noted Zionist,[2] Peter Beinart, columnist for *The Atlantic* and *Haaretz*: "What sort of state faces an existential threat by merely respecting the human rights of those whose lives it governs?" and "Is that really the kind of state that you want to support?"[5]

The more you practice, the better you will become. By going through this process, I have learned a lot about myself and others. I wish you success in learning about your own and your conversation partners' positions. I hope you and they enjoy the learning experience and that you develop meaningful personal connections. Remain true to your values and ethics, and help your partners do the same.

---

2   Peter Beinart's position on Israel and Zionism changed in 2020.

I hope this guide and its queries will be food for thought, discovery, and connection. The Israel/Palestine conflict is not likely to be resolved if people can't even communicate concepts precisely and accurately. Communication requires a shared language, vocabulary, values, and understanding. I hope this *When They Speak Israel* guide will be a tool for you to bridge that understanding.

GROUP 1:
Attacking You

Group 1 includes three Israel expressions that in effect are attacking you:

1. **"That comment is so anti-Semitic."** This statement implies that *you* are an anti-Semite.

2. **"Why are you singling out Israel?"** This question implies that you are biased by treating Israel differently from other countries.

3. **"This view is not balanced; it is pro-Palestinian."** This statement implies that you are biased by being pro-Palestinian.

Understand that they are accusing you because they are on the defensive. As long as you are against all forms of racism, then you cannot be anti-Jewish and you cannot be pro-Palestinian; you are pro-equality. Breathe. It's about them, not about you—whether they know it or not.

1. "That Comment Is So Anti-Semitic."

Similar Expressions:

▸ "Criticism of Israel is anti-Semitic (anti-Jewish)."

▸ "Anti-Zionism is anti-Semitic."

▸ "You are an anti-Semite!" or "You are a self-hating Jew!"

Related Facts:

There are multiple definitions of anti-Semitism:

- Merriam-Webster defines *anti-Semitism* as "feeling or showing hostility toward or discrimination against Jews as a cultural, racial, or ethnic group."[6]

- The International Holocaust Remembrance Alliance (IHRA)'s working definition of *anti-Semitism* is: "Antisemitism is a certain perception of Jews, which may be expressed as hatred toward Jews. Rhetorical and physical manifestations of antisemitism are directed toward Jewish or non-Jewish individuals and/or their property, toward Jewish community institutions and religious facilities."[7] Unlike the Merriam-Webster definition, the IHRA's definition is vague and unclear.

Since 2016, pro-Israel groups have been increasingly successful at convincing governments and educational institutions in the United States and around the world to adopt the IHRA's definition of anti-Semitism even though it is self-described as a "non-legally binding working definition." Maybe because the working definition is ambiguous, the

IHRA has included examples that "may serve as illustrations."

A number of these examples mention Israel including: "Manifestations [of anti-Semitism] might include the targeting of the state of Israel, conceived as a Jewish collectivity." Examples like this one are used to protect Israel from criticism of its racist policies. Even the author of the definition, Dr. Kenneth Stern, Ph.D., has spoken out against its current use to stifle legitimate speech.[8]

Anti-Semitism, which historically has been a form of racism, is suddenly flipped on its head. It is now used as a tool to practice racism rather than fight against it—by calling those who stand for equality anti-Semitic while protecting from criticism those who stand for Jewish supremacy in Israel/Palestine.

Typically, individuals and institutions which push for or use the IHRA definition as a weapon to stifle speech actually misstate the definition. Even though the previously mentioned example about Israel does not fit under this qualification, the majority of the "working definition" examples are qualified by the working definition stating that they "could, taking into account the overall context" be anti-Semitic. If someone cites the IHRA definition to "prove" that a particular remark or action critical of Israel or Zionism is anti-Semitic, pay attention to whether the person presenting the "proof" has "tak[en] into account the overall context." It is rare that those who use the IHRA definition as a weapon will have done so.

Adding the caveat that the examples need to be taken into context to determine if in fact they are anti-Semitic means that the examples themselves are not conclusive. The IHRA definition therefore remains ambiguous and subjective and the examples inconclusive. When having conversations about Israel and the accusation of anti-Semitism arises, require a clear and unambiguous definition; without clarity, words and expressions do not help mutual understanding.

- William Marr, a German journalist and political activist who discriminated against Jews, popularized the term *anti-Semitism* in the late nineteenth century as a way to distinguish hatred of Jews as an ethnic group as opposed to hatred of Jews as a religious group. The term was therefore developed as a tool for promoting racism. Over time, Jews have used the term to fight discrimination against them, turning what Marr had considered a positive trait into a negative trait. The IHRA definition now further transforms the term from being one used to fight racism back to a meaning that actually condones racism—this time against Palestinians.

- Merriam-Webster defines *Semite* as "a member of any of a number of peoples of ancient southwestern Asia including the Akkadians, Phoenicians, Hebrews, and Arabs."[9] Some Arabs consider the term *anti-Semitic* offensive, since its accepted definition discriminates against non-Jewish Semites.

Unpacking the Israel Language:

The implied narratives underlying the statement "That comment is so anti-Semitic" include the following:

▸ The definition of *anti-Semitism* is clear and universal.

▸ All accusations of *anti-Semitism* condemn racism.

Unfortunately, both of these implied narratives are false. The IHRA definition includes criticism of Israel, thereby conflating any criticism of state policies with hostility toward an ethnic group. Accusing someone of anti-Semitism when they are standing for equality condones rather than condemns racism.

If we translate the Israel statement "Anti-Zionism is anti-Semitism" into English, the result is "Opposition to Israel as a Jewish privileged state (anti-Zionism) is to be discriminatory against, or hateful to, Jews (anti-Semitism)." Unpacking the statement yields: "The only way not to be racist against Jews is to be racist against someone else."

The Core Issue:

If standing for equality is defined to be anti-Semitic, then *anti-Semitism* is defined to protect Jewish privilege. Standing for equality is not racism; it is anti-racism.

Recommended Approach:

1. **Don't worry; being accused of being anti-Semitic does not mean you are racist.**

   Many people avoid talking about Israel/Palestine in public because they fear they'll be accused of being anti-Semitic. If you are knowledgeable about the situation and effective in shining a light on the issues, you will most likely be called anti-Semitic. It is to be expected, even for those of us who oppose all forms of discrimination and racism. It is to be expected because that has been a tactic used by Zionists to silence opposition.

   Here is one of the reasons we know that this technique is used to protect Israel rather than to protect Jews: Equality supporters who oppose Israeli policies are often called anti-Semites, yet Christian Zionists who want Jews to move to Israel so that they can die in the Rapture rarely face that accusation.

2. **Check to make sure that you are standing for equality.**

   Make sure you are against all forms of racism (discrimination against anyone based on ethnicity, descent, or country of origin). If you can look in the mirror knowing you stand for equality, then you will know that any accusation directed toward you of any form of racism is false. It is most important that you are conscious of your stand for equality and human rights for all because aggressors aren't always after the truth; they want to control the conversation and make you feel vulnerable.

Once you have checked yourself and confirmed that what you said, or the position you supported, was based on equality, then you can choose how to formulate your response. If you have not gone through this process, however, your response will be defensive and lead to self-doubt.

3. **Understand why your conversation partner made the statement.**

Someone might accuse you of being anti-Semitic because they believe that you said something discriminatory or hateful, but some people use the accusation to silence opposition. Just because someone believes a statement is anti-Semitic doesn't mean that the statement is discriminatory, racist, or hateful. That is because different definitions of *anti-Semitism* conflict.

A definition of *anti-Semitism* that includes criticism of Israel implies that Israel belongs to Jews. Implying that a country belongs preferentially to one ethnic group over another is racist, especially when the indigenous population is discriminated against. (This guide covers the notion of Israel being Jewish in more detail in the discussion under Israel language expression number 4, "Do you believe Israel has the right to exist?")

Before responding to an anti-Semitism accusation, ask which definition your conversation partner is using. You can also ask: "What precisely about that statement made it anti-Semitic?" If the statement was critical of the state or its policies, then it is not inherently racist, just as criticizing Egypt or Saudi Arabia is not inherently anti-Arab.

If your conversation partner responds with a statement related to Israel being Jewish, then follow up with a question such as "How is criticism of Israel anti-Jewish?" Ultimately, they will get to the point where they may say, "Well, it's the Jewish state, and criticism of Israel is criticism of Jews." Following are a number of queries to ponder with your partner:

- ❷ "How is a position discriminatory when it is standing for equality and condemning racial discrimination?"

- ❷ "Why do you choose to interpret support for equality as anti-Jewish?"

- ❷ "What concerns you more: someone calling equality anti-Jewish or someone calling a racist state Jewish? Why?"

4. **Reach clarity and understanding.**

   a. **Confirm that your conversation partner is also against all forms of racism and that they support equality for all.**

   If they answer that they are against all forms of racism (ethnic discrimination), then ask them such questions as "If you support equality for all, then why do you think it is anti-Jewish to criticize Israel's racist policies?"

They may come back with a statement I have heard numerous times: "Yes, but you are not treating Israel equally. There are many other countries that violate human rights." Responses might include the following:

❷ "Are you suggesting that we don't criticize any country's human rights record without criticizing all human rights violators simultaneously? Do you criticize any country's human rights? What criteria do you use to determine whether you criticize a country for human rights violations?"

❷ "What is the most appropriate response to a country that systematically violates human rights in order to maintain ethnic supremacy?"

❷ "How do we refrain from being complicit in human rights violations in countries that we have supported for decades financially, militarily, and politically?"

❷ "Are you asking me not to criticize Israel for its human rights violations? If so, what criteria do you use to decide which human-rights-violating countries to defend by protecting them from criticism?"

Who knows, they may have a good response. But if they don't, it is important that defenders of oppression know that you are aware that they are defending oppression and that you are willing to call it out.

If your conversation partner is not against all forms of racism and they say that discrimination against Palestinians is appropriate because the Palestinians are terrorists, you can ask them what they think of stereotyping ethnic groups.

b. Confirm that your conversation partner understands that Israel is a racist state.

Meaningful conversations cannot occur without some common understanding. The most basic issue is that Israel is a racist state; it gives one ethnic group preferential treatment at the expense of another ethnic group. If your partner does not believe that Israel gives preferential treatment to one ethnic group over another, then the easiest example to highlight is citizenship. Israel discriminates against everyone in the world—except about fifteen million people. That is because Israel has a "Law of Return," which allows Jews, because of their ethnicity or religion, to become a citizen within forty-eight hours of arriving in Israel. (This 1950 Israeli "Law of Return" should not be confused with the international Right of Return, which Israel denies to Palestinians.)

If your conversation partner is unaware of this Israeli law, then have them look it up. The law discriminates against anyone who is not

Jewish, whether that person is White, African American, Asian American, or Latinx. By having this conversation with an Israel supporter, you can make the conversation more personal. For example, you can ask, "Why is it OK for Israel, the largest recipient of our foreign aid, to be racist against me?"

Of course, Israel's discrimination against Palestinians is much worse. Citizenship is given in forty-eight hours to Jews who cannot name a single relative who ever lived there, whereas Palestinians who have the deed to their homes, can name their grandparents and the village they lived in, and are registered refugees are not allowed to return.

As obviously racist as this may appear to many, the Israel messaging is so pervasive that many Zionists don't see a problem with it. They may react with "What do you expect? It's a Jewish state." A number of responses to this are appropriate, but one that highlights the point is "Good, we agree that a Jewish state is racist."

Because the Israel messaging is so powerful, many have regarded Israel as "defending Jews" rather than as "being racist." One can defend Jews, and all minorities, with a strong constitution. One can defend minorities with laws requiring equality. But Israel "defends Jews" by violating Palestinian human rights. This distinction is not part of the Israel messaging.

Your conversation partner may be confused or may realize that they have been bamboozled. They have been taught that anti-Zionism was discriminatory, even though it isn't, and they may have been taught that defending Jews by supporting Zionism was not racist, even though it actually is. This is the power of the Israel language framing. If your partner is feeling confused or bamboozled, be sensitive. Give them time and space. They are facing a very difficult situation. You don't want to embarrass them in public. They do, however, need to know that it is obvious that they are on the wrong side of justice. In this case, it is obvious that they are supporting a racist position while accusing someone else of being racist for standing for equality. Good friends tell their friends bad news in a loving way.

Sample Queries to Engage Your Conversation Partner:

❷ "Please help me understand how standing for equality is racist against anyone."

❷ "If one labels standing for equality as anti-Semitic, then does that not open the dangerous door of anti-Semitism being a moral stand, a position that can only lead to violence?"

2. "Why Are You Singling Out Israel?"

Similar Expressions:

▶ "Why are you picking on Israel? Why are you making Israel the exception?"

▶ "You are anti-Semitic because you are picking on Israel."

▶ "Do you criticize all countries that violate human rights?"

Related Facts:

• Israel regularly restricts human rights organizations, including the UN, from assessing Israel's human rights record.[10] Israel has denied both Human Rights Watch and Amnesty International personnel access to the occupied territories.[11]

• Israel is the only country in the world that systematically arrests, detains, interrogates, and tries children under military law, between five hundred and seven hundred per year.[12]

  • 54 percent are taken from their beds at home in the middle of the night;

  • 97 percent are interrogated without a family member, 69 percent of them are not properly informed of their rights;

  • 85 percent are blindfolded when they are kidnapped by the Israeli military, and 72 percent of them experience physical violence;

  • and 56 percent end up signing documents in Hebrew, a language most of them don't understand.[13]

In 2019, H.R. 2407 was introduced in the US House of Representatives to combat Israel's violations of children's rights. It followed H.R. 4391 introduced in 2017.

- Until 2015, Israel was the cause of the largest number of refugees in the world,[14] and for more than seventy years, it has continued to deny them their right to return to their homeland.

- Amnesty International released a report in 2016 of the top ten countries with the worst human rights records: China, Egypt, Gambia, Hungary, Israel, Kenya, Pakistan, Russia, Saudi Arabia, and Syria.[15]

- Israel has historically been the largest recipient of US foreign aid, amounting to more than $3 billion per year.[16] The United States is in violation of our own "Leahy laws," which prohibit "the US government from using funds for assistance to units of foreign security forces where there is credible information implicating that unit in the commission of gross violations of human rights."[17]

Unpacking the Israel Language:

The false implied narratives underlying the question "Why are you singling out Israel?" include the following:

▸ Focusing on Israel's crimes is unfair or inappropriate.

▸ You are criticizing only Israel for human rights violations.

▸ You, rather than those accusing you, are singling out Israel.

▸ Singling out Israel is racist against Jews.

This accusation of singling out Israel is a distraction because I don't know of anyone who criticizes only Israel for its human rights violations. You may criticize only Israel in one conversation, but in other conversations, you may criticize only North Korea or focus only on the mistreatment of African Americans. Just because Israel happens to be the only country mentioned in a particular conversation does not mean that you are accusing only Israel of human rights violations.

The accusers are actually more likely to be the ones singling out Israel. How many other countries are they protecting from human rights violation critics?

The Core Issue:

The argument that you are singling out Israel is actually a self-reflection and a distraction by your conversation partner.

It is a self-reflection because *they* single out Israel by defending only Israel's crimes (*unless they also defend other countries that violated human rights*).

It is a distraction because it is perfectly appropriate for us to hold our number-one recipient of foreign aid and number-one beneficiary of our UN Security Council vetoes responsible for its human rights violations so that we are not complicit in its crimes.[18]

Recommended Approach:

Do not get bogged down with the singling-out issue. It's a distraction. It's an effort to put you on the defensive. Understand that your conversation partner is asking you why you are picking on a human rights violator. The question needs to be turned around; your partner needs to explain why they are defending a human rights violator.

The first step would be to confirm that your partner knows that Israel is a human rights violator and that it is racist. You can do a simple validation by asking the following question:

❷ "Do you know that Israel has denied Palestinians equal rights, including citizenship and the international Right of Return, for more than seventy years?"

If they respond that they are not aware of this discrimination, then ask them what a "Jewish state" means. At some point that conversation will likely lead to ethnic preferential treatment, otherwise known as racism.

If they respond that they are aware of denied Palestinian rights but again ask why you are picking on Israel, then you can ask them how many human-rights-violating countries do they defend.

Israel's double standard has been supported for so long that people accept it as normal. With it has come the double standard that it is OK for Jews to discriminate against Palestinians, but no one is allowed to discriminate against Jews. I told a Jewish Zionist friend that I was totally fine with him choosing to support racism (the state of Israel). I asked him just not to be a hypocrite. I asked him therefore to never accuse anyone else of racism, including anti-Semitism, while he supported racism. I told him that having a friend be racist is one thing, but his being a hypocrite is pushing it! Occasional humor can relieve stress when we're dealing with a topic as heavy as Israel/Palestine.

Sample Query to Engage Your Conversation Partner:

❷ "You're right! Let's quit singling out Israel. You stop singling out Israel by protecting it from its crimes, and let's get back to the human rights violations of [*pick one of the following*]:

 ❷ our number-one recipient of foreign aid, which is reported to be one of the ten worst human rights violators."[19]

 ❷ the only country that systematically incarcerates children under a military system violating their human rights."[20]

 ❷ the country that has historically created the largest number of refugees."[3][21]

 ❷ ..."

---

3   See the preceding footnote about there now being more Syrian than Palestinian refugees.

3. "This View Is Not Balanced; It Is Pro-Palestinian."

Similar Expressions:

▸ "This article/book/lecture/conversation needs to include more of the Israeli perspective."

▸ "This perspective does not take into sufficient account Jewish history of persecution and the Holocaust."

Related Facts:

• We need to define *balance*. The word can mean different things to different people. The following are some questions you can ask yourself to clarify what balance means to you; they may also be helpful with your conversation partner:

  • "Is 'balance' an equal coverage of two perspectives, or is it balancing the rights of all people?"

  • "What is a balanced perspective of whether or not the Earth is flat?"

  • "How would you discuss slavery in a balanced way?"

  • "What is the balanced discussion on the 1948/1949 Berlin Blockade?" (The answer to this question might be helpful in knowing how to have a conversation with your partner about the Israeli blockade of Gaza.)

• There is no balance in a military occupation or a blockade against civilians.

• There is no balance in violations of human rights.

- There is no balance in the taking of land by force.

- There is no balance in systemic and institutional racist legal systems.

- There is no balance in military attacks against a civilian population.

- If pro-equality is called pro-Palestinian, then pro-Israel is anti-equality.

Unpacking the Israel Language:

The argument that your position is not balanced, that pro-equality is pro-Palestinian, has unspoken narratives and assumptions. They may include one or more of the assertions in the following list. You may have others that are not listed. Go through the list and highlight which ones resonate with you and your conversation partner:

▶ that balance is possible, especially in an unbalanced situation

▶ that balance is appropriate in an unbalanced situation

▶ that standing for equality is not balanced (since your conversation partner is calling it "pro-Palestinian")

▶ that your partner wants balance

Be careful, some of these positions may seem to be contradictory. For example, you can sound conflicting if you say that one can't have balance in an unbalanced situation while also saying that equality is balanced. Here is the distinction: A balanced position would be for all people to have equal rights but not to give oppressors time equal to that given to victims. Victims deserve preferential consideration over oppressors.

The Core Issues:

Pro-equality is not pro-Palestinian, just as it is not pro-Jewish.

Pro-equality is anti-racism.

Zionists call anti-racism "pro-Palestinian," which implies that "pro-Israel" requires racial discrimination.

When they say, "This view is not balanced; it is pro-Palestinian," what they really mean is "Your position for equal rights is balanced, and that is a problem for Zionists."

Recommended Approach:

This is another case of Zionist accusers projecting what they themselves are doing. They are not balanced and don't intend to be. They are trying to distract you and put you on the defensive because they are not balanced.

You could get into a conversation about balance and ask what "balance" means in an oppressive occupation in which human rights are violated. Unfortunately, taking the conversation in that direction will only prove that they are not balanced and that they have never wanted balance. If Zionists had wanted balance, they would have asked for Palestinian input before they lobbied for the Balfour Declaration in 1917. If they had wanted balance, they would not have assassinated Lord Moyne, the British leader of the House of Lords and secretary of state for the colonies, in 1944, when he was coming up with a partition plan for Palestine. There are many more examples, but the bottom line is if Zionists supported balance, they would support humanitarian law and equality. Racism is never balanced.

The most productive approach to the "balance" accusation is to again focus on the main issue and foundational problem with Zionism: racism. Therefore, your response needs to be something that leads the conversation back to racism and to exposing Israel—and your conversation partner's support for Israel—as supporting racism.

Sample Queries to Return the Discussion to Racism:

❷ "I want to understand what you mean by balance. How do you recommend we have a balanced conversation about a state that requires racism to maintain its identity?" (If your conversation partner comes up with a rationalization for racism, then ask, "If racism is acceptable in such a situation, then are you equally OK with a country being racist against Jews?")

❷ "If your view is that equal rights for Jews and Palestinians is not balanced, then are you saying that balance is achievable only by violating human rights?

Are you as OK with those rights being violated against Jews as you are against Palestinians?"

❷ "What is a balanced perspective on violations of human rights and crimes against humanity?" (Such as with South African apartheid, the Armenian Genocide, the Holocaust, the Darfur massacre, the Israeli occupation, etc.).

❷ "When other countries—such as Saudi Arabia or China—are criticized for violating human rights, do you also ask for a balanced perspective of their oppressions?"

❷ "When someone promotes or speaks well of Israel, do you ask for a balancing position?"

❷ If pro-equality is pro-Palestinian, then how can pro-Israel be anything other than anti-equality or pro-racism?"

❷ "When you say this perspective is not balanced because it does not put enough emphasis on the Israeli perspective, what specifically is missing? What is missing other than a rationalization for ethnic (Jewish) supremacy and discrimination?"

❷ "If you think more of the Israeli perspective is needed, what do you suggest we add?"

   ❷ "Justification for racist laws and multiple legal systems?"

   ❷ "Support for the violation of indigenous equal rights (including self-determination)?"

   ❷ "Defense for ethnic cleansing of indigenous people from the land?"

❷ "Complicity in the erasure of a people's history from the land?"

❷ "Are you suggesting that it is appropriate to use the Holocaust as a justification for racial discrimination, ethnic cleansing, violating human rights, war crimes, and crimes against humanity?"

GROUP 2:
Pressuring Acceptance of a Jewish State

Group 2 includes three Israel expressions that in effect are pressuring you to accept a Jewish state:

4. **"Do you believe Israel has the right to exist?"**

5. **"The world community (UN) gave Jews Israel because of the Holocaust."**

6. **"But God gave Jews the land."**

In effect, these expressions are saying, "God and the international community have stood for a Jewish state. What about you?"

Stay true to anti-racism. If your conversation partner chooses to interpret scripture in a certain way and based on that interpretation chooses to believe in a God who is racist, then that is their choice. Their believing that the international community supports racism does not make their belief true or the international community right. And if they believe that supporting an ethnic state that needs to be racist in order to survive reflects Jewish values, then who is really anti-Jewish?

4. "Do You Believe Israel Has the Right to Exist?"

Similar Expressions:

▶ "Do you think a Jewish state has the right to exist?"

▶ "Jews have never had a homeland. Don't they deserve one?"

▶ "If Jews don't have Israel, then where will they be safe?"

▶ "Ending the Jewish state will lead to a genocide of Jews."

Related Facts:

• The 1917 Balfour Declaration, while supporting the establishment of a national home for the Jewish people, asserted that "it being clearly understood that nothing shall be done which may prejudice the civil and religious rights of existing non-Jewish communities in Palestine."[22]

• Within the 1947 UN Resolution 181 ("Plan of Partition with Economic Union"), Part I ("Future Constitution and Government of Palestine"), are the following provisions:[23]

  • Under "B. Steps Preparatory to Independence," item number 10: "The constitutions of the States shall … include *inter alia* provisions for … (d) Guaranteeing to all persons equal and non-discriminatory rights in civil, political, economic and religious matters and the enjoyment of human rights and fundamental freedoms, including freedom of religion, language, speech and publication, education, assembly and association."

- Under "C. Declaration," Chapter 2, "Religious and Minority Rights," including the following items:

  - "2. No discrimination of any kind shall be made between the inhabitants on the ground of race, religion, language or sex."

  - "3. All persons within the jurisdiction of the State shall be entitled to equal protection of the laws."

- Nation states are a relatively new phenomenon. Not all ethnicities have a nation state. For example, the Inuit people of North America don't have a nation state. States that used to be considered ethnic (France, Germany, etc.) are now multiracial and interracial. Does the concept of an ethnic state really lead to long term peace?

Unpacking the Israel Language:

The wording of the question "Do you believe Israel has the right to exist?" is disingenuous. It is disingenuous because it

▸ Makes the issue of Israel's right to exist a belief (by using the word *believe*). The wording subconsciously connects in a religious way to Christians and other "believers."

▸ Does not define Israel. It allows the questioner to change their definition after you have answered the question. Israel can be a piece of land (although the state of Israel has never defined its borders). Israel can also be a Jewish state giving preferential treatment to one ethnic group while discriminating against another. Finally, Israel can be a combination of these: a racist state that can choose its boundaries at will.

▶ Usurps individuals' rights and gives them to a government. In the case of Israel, this language gives the state a "right" to violate human rights.

▶ Encourages a positive answer with the word *exist*. If the state did not have the "right to exist," then how would it exist today?

Take your time answering tricky questions such as this. You need to be aware of their implications and traps.

The Core Issue:

It is important to get validation and clarification from your conversation partner, but usually the question "Do you believe that Israel has the right to exist?" is a disingenuous way of asking if you support a state that gives preferential rights to one ethnic group (Jews) at the expense of another (Palestinians).

In other words, will you sign on to their petition for a racist state?

Recommended Approach:

Because the language is so tricky—and your conversation partner may not even realize it is tricky—it is best to make sure you both are on the same page. Confirm that your partner is asking you if you support a state that gives preferential rights to one ethnic group at the expense of another.

To get validation and clarification from your conversation partner, walk through those steps as questions:

1. "When you ask if I believe Israel has the right to exist, are you asking me if I support a Jewish state?"

2. "Does that mean you are asking me if I support a state that gives preferential rights to one ethnic group—Jews in this case—at the expense of another ethnic group?"

3. "So, you are asking me if I would support a racist state? Do you support racist states?"

Sample Queries to Engage Your Conversation Partner on Whether Safety Can Come through Oppression:

If your conversation partner brings up the issue of safety for the Jewish people—either as a reason for a Jewish state or as a justification for Jewish supremacy—then you can respond with questions like:

❷ "Do you believe that violating other people's rights makes the oppressor safer or less safe—especially over the long term?"

❷ "How does taking more land from Palestinians, as Israel did in 1967, make Israeli Jews safer?"

❷ "Are you OK with ethnically cleansing the land of Palestinians to make Jews safer? If so, are you also OK with similar ethnic cleansing of Jews to make Palestinians safer?"

❷ "If Jews want to be a majority in order to maintain democratic control, then why would they want to take more Palestinian-populated land?"

❷ "Why do Jews need to violate others' human rights in order to feel safe? Would Jews not be safer by advocating for human rights across the globe?"

5. "The World Community (UN) Gave Jews Israel because of the Holocaust."

Similar Expressions:

▶ "The Balfour Declaration and the UN-approved Partition Plan documented the right for a Jewish state to exist."

▶ "The world community through the UN gave Jews Israel."

Related Facts:

- The 1917 British Balfour Declaration,[24] which pledged a Jewish homeland in Palestine, preceded the Holocaust by two decades. It was the Balfour Declaration that led to the British Mandate of Palestine and the subsequent mass immigration of Jews to Palestine, all starting decades before the Holocaust.

- The United Kingdom through the Balfour Declaration and Mandate, abetted by the United States in putting together the UN Partition Plan, proceeded against the right of self-determination of the people of Palestine.

- In April 1947, five UN member states (Egypt, Iraq, Lebanon, Saudi Arabia, and Syria) requested that the following be placed on the agenda: "the termination of the mandate over Palestine and the declaration of its independence."[25] That request was denied. Instead, the UN moved forward to develop a plan to partition.

- In 1947, the United States threatened countries that their foreign aid would cease if they did not vote for the UN Partition Plan.

- UN Resolution 181, approving the Partition Plan on November 29, 1947 ("Plan of Partition with Economic Union"), Part I ("Future Constitution and Government of Palestine"), B. Steps Preparatory to Independence," item number 10, stipulated the following:

> The constitutions of the States shall ... include *inter alia* provisions for ... (d) Guaranteeing to all persons equal and non-discriminatory rights in civil, political, economic and religious matters and the enjoyment of human rights and fundamental freedoms, including freedom of religion, language, speech and publication, education, assembly and association.[26]

Unpacking the Israel Language:

The statement "The world community (UN) gave Jews Israel because of the Holocaust" implies

▸ that the world community agreed to take one person's land and give it to someone else

▸ that the UN can go against its charter of supporting the self-determination of people

▸ that the land the state of Israel controls today is the land that the UN approved as the Jewish state in the 1947 Partition Plan

▸ that the world community approved a racist state with Jewish privilege at Palestinian expense

▸ that the Holocaust justifies a racist state

Of course, these implied Israel messages are false. As with any deception, the statement contains a grain of truth. The grain of truth is the following: The UN did approve Resolution 181, which divided Palestine and approved a state that had slightly more Jews than Arabs and was referred to as the "Jewish state." What is missing from the messaging, however, is that the resolution called for two states, including one referred to as the "Arab state," as well as an international zone (Jerusalem).

The messaging also leaves out that none of the borders between the "Jewish state" and the "Arab state" of the UN Partition Plan were ever actually established, meaning that "Israel" has always included part of the Arab state and international zone of Jerusalem. In other words, Resolution 181 was never implemented.

Claiming that the Holocaust caused the UN to give the Jews Israel in 1947 is also misleading because that process had started in 1917 with the Balfour Declaration and was being implemented throughout the period of the British Mandate, for more than a quarter century before the end of World War II.

The Israel language statement is also misleading because the UN did not "give" the Jews Israel; rather, it approved the creation of a state that was slightly more than half Jewish, and it required that each new state guarantee "all persons equal and non-discriminatory rights in civil, political, economic and religious matters." When it comes to Israel, all persons have never had equal and non-discriminatory rights.

The argument of UN approval attempts to create the false illusion of international consent of Israel possessing the land that it occupies and of an Israeli state that gives preferential rights to Jews at the expense of the native people. The opposite is true. The UN has passed numerous resolutions condemning Israel's taking of the land by force, creating a refugee disaster, and violating Palestinian human rights.

The Core Issue:

The UN did not approve a racist state, and nothing justifies a racist state.

Using the Holocaust, a horrible and racist murder of millions of people, as justification for further racism is unsettling.

If racist violations of human rights are an acceptable response, then what was the problem with the initial racist violations?

Is the severity the only issue, or are they all crimes?

Recommended Approach and Sample Queries:

Keep bringing the conversation back to Israel's being a racist state while developing your relationship and trying to understand your conversation partner's assumptions. Here are some possible queries:

❷ "Are you suggesting that the UN supports the violation of human rights, war crimes, and crimes against humanity? Are you suggesting that the UN supports Israel to maintain itself as a Jewish state on the land it now controls?"

❷ "Do you believe that the United Nations approved a state that requires violating human rights in order to maintain its identity? If so, which resolution did so (since Resolution 181 does not meet that criteria)?"

The argument that the international community gave Jews the land is problematic because it is a violation of both the self-determination and the human rights of those who have lived on the land for many centuries. Here are some related queries:

❷ "If Zionists took control of Palestine by force after World War II, then are they legitimate rulers?"

❷ "Since the state of Israel confiscated land from people whose rights it violated, is that not stealing? To whom does stolen property belong?"

❷ "Who has the right to take away self-determination? Is it OK to claim the need for Jewish self-determination at the expense of Palestinian self-determination?"

Only if you are very familiar with United Nations resolutions, you may want to ask the following questions:

❷ "When did Israel adopt the borders or constitutional requirements of equal treatment of Arabs and Jews included in the 1947 General Assembly Resolution 181? When did Israel comply with the 1948 General Assembly Resolution 194 or the 1967 Security Council Resolution 242?" (The answer is never.)

❷ "If Israel can be rationalized by one UN resolution, then what about the international laws and many UN resolutions that Israel violates?"

6. "But God Gave Jews the Land."

Similar Expressions:

▸ "The Bible says that the land belongs to the Jews."

▸ "God made a covenant to the Jews, giving them the land of Israel."

▸ "If God didn't give Israel to the Jews, then why is it called 'the Promised Land'?"

▸ "The people of Israel were God's Chosen People, so are you sure you want to argue about this?"

Related Facts:

• A number of Jewish, Christian, and Muslim organizations strongly dispute Scripture interpretation that grants to ethnic Jews exclusive and unconditional rights to the land. The Vatican, for example, recognizes the state of Palestine.[27] Ten United States denominations have even gone beyond criticizing Israel; they are participating in the Boycott, Divestment and Sanctions (BDS) movement, which calls for the end of the Israeli occupation, for equal rights for Palestinians, and for honoring Palestinians' right to return to their homeland.[28]

• The Bible also states that "you will quickly perish from the good land He has given you" when you "serve other gods"[29] or when you no longer "keep the way of the Lord."[30] Such passages would lead one to question an unconditional and eternal grant.

• Israel today is a portion of the land of Israel described in the Bible. They are not the same.

Unpacking the Israel Language:

"But God gave Jews the land" is based on the following assumptions and unspoken narratives:

▶ The idea of God giving the land to Jews is a fact rather than a belief. (A more accurate statement might be "I believe God gave Jews the land.")

▶ There is only one God, and everyone chooses to believe in the same God. (A more accurate statement might be "My God gave Jews the land" or "The Evangelical Christian God gave Jews the land" or "One of the Hindu gods gave Jews the land.")

▶ The Bible reflects only God's will, unambiguously communicates God's will, and has never been influenced by any man or woman in its writing, compilation, and translations.

▶ God gave the land exclusively and for eternity to ethnic Jews and religious Jews, including those who deviate from His laws.

▶ "The land" referred to is the land that today's state of Israel controls rather than the land described in the Bible, which some say includes all of today's Israel, Palestine, Jordan, and Lebanon, plus parts of Syria, Iraq, Saudi Arabia, Kuwait, and Egypt.

The problem with these assumptions is that, at best, they are beliefs and, at worst, some can be disproven or are illogical. If one is a Christian and accepts the Bible as God's Word, then one has to accept the following commandment: "So, in everything, do to others what you would have them do to you, for this sums up the Law and the Prophets."[31]

This guide is not a religious document, and I am not a religious scholar. However, some laws of conscience and logic are universal. It is illogical, on the one hand, to claim that God is a loving God and wants us to treat one another as we would want to be treated while also, on the other hand, claiming that He wants us to ethnically cleanse a land of one ethnic group and violate their human rights as we make another group supreme in the land.

Another passage warns: "Watch out for false prophets. They come to you in sheep's clothing, but inwardly they are ferocious wolves. By their fruit you will recognize them."[32] Ethnic cleansing of a land is bad fruit; any racism is bad fruit.

If Jesus said that to treat people as you would want to be treated (equality) sums up the Law of the Prophets, then how can one also claim that God supports ethnic discrimination (racism)?

You may want to ask your conversation partner how they resolve these conflicting concepts and values. Be aware that beliefs are deep in our psyches. This topic will likely need a great deal of care, listening, empathy, and time.

> # The Core Issue:
> Whom we choose as our God:
>
> - Do we choose to believe in a God Who wants us to see that all people, or just some people, are made in God's image?
>
> - Do we choose to believe in a God Who is loving to all people, or a racist god?

How each of us, including your conversation partner, answers these core issue questions affects how each of us lives our life. If we choose to believe in a racist god, then how can we not end up racist as well?

Recommended Approach:

The concept of God giving land to the Jews can be a difficult one to discuss with your conversation partner if that partner believes their faith is truth. No one chooses to believe things that they know are false; however, it is a problem when people convince themselves that their unprovable leap of faith is undeniable truth. The conviction is even more problematical when they believe that other leaps of faith are false. Faith is faith. Truth is truth. If faith were provable, it would no longer be faith.

Challenging one's beliefs is difficult for many people. Even if your conversation partner is willing to accept that their beliefs are a choice, that they chose their religion, and therefore that they chose that religion's corresponding image of God(s), they may not be willing to look too closely at their beliefs. You therefore need to focus very clearly on the issues that might raise questions but not dwell on this subject.

For example, you might ask them if their God supports racism; why or why not? If they accept God as supporting racism, then you can ask them if it is not logical then that others should equally be able to believe in a God that promotes racism even if that racism is directed against them. You might want to ask them how that makes them feel.

On a high level, I recommend that you acknowledge that you understand that your partner believes the Israel language expression to be true but that you don't (assuming that you don't believe that the expression is true). And further, that you would really like to understand the implications of their belief on this issue.

I strongly recommend that you not get involved in the religious texts. As I mentioned in the introduction, the purpose of this guide is to help you develop relationships with Zionists and to understand their perspectives while asking them to explain discrepancies in the logic of their positions. Again, this is not a guide for helping you argue; that would require extensive knowledge and practice. Needless to say, experts disagree on religious interpretations, so what does any single interpretation prove? The problem with going down a religious text and interpretation path is that there is no exit. The best you could hope for is proving that there are different interpretations of the Bible, and that is not helpful. The question to ask your partner is what values they stand for.

Focus on conversations that deal with the primary issue (racism) and this guide's two objectives: (a) to develop a relationship with your conversation partner and (b) to better understand both your own perspective and your partner's. There are two conversation topics that will most quickly get you to the core issue:

1. What are the consequences of your partner's beliefs? If they choose selective parts of the Bible that lead them to believe that God gave the biblical land of Israel to blood descendants (as opposed to exclusively spiritual descendants) at the expense of other peoples, then what does it say about their God's stand on racism? What does it say about what they see as right, ethical, and holy relative to the ethnic cleansing of the land?

2. Why do they choose to believe in a God that would want to ethnically cleanse much of the Middle East? How is that a God of love? How can one love one's neighbors as oneself, consider everyone to be in the image of God, and care for the downtrodden—while at the same time, one is ethnically cleansing human beings and violating human rights, as the state of Israel has been doing for more than seventy years?

Sample Queries to Learn How Your Conversation Partner Looks at Ethics, Racism, and God:

❷ "How would you explain to a Hindu or Buddhist that God gave the land to the Jews?"

❷ "If God gives land exclusively to one ethnic group for eternity at the expense of other peoples, then does that not make God racist?"

❷ "How can we condemn anyone for ethnic discrimination (racism) if it is acceptable in God's eyes?"

❷ "If God gave biblical Israel to the Jews exclusively, then do you promote getting rid of all non-Jews in all of today's Israel, Palestine, Jordan, and Lebanon, plus parts of Syria, Iraq, Saudi Arabia, Kuwait, and Egypt?"

  ❷ "If not, then why only ethnically cleanse Palestine?"

  ❷ "If not, then why not create Israel where there are fewer people and where ethnic cleansing would not be necessary?"

  ❷ "Either God gave the Jews all the land of biblical Israel, or God didn't. Which is it?"

GROUP 3:
Justifying Israeli Actions

Group 3 includes three Israel expressions that attempt to justify Israeli actions:

7. **"Doesn't Israel have the right to defend itself (against Palestinian violence and terrorism)?"**

8. **"Israel has always had to defend itself from aggressive Arab nations."**

9. **"The Security Fence/Wall/Barrier is needed to protect Israel."**

Remember that *defense* is an oft-used word in the Israel language. But Zionists took the land by force, so how is that defensive? What is defensive about a fifty-plus-year occupation? When it blocks human rights, including the international Right of Return, Israel is being offensive.

7. "Doesn't Israel Have the Right to Defend Itself (against Palestinian Violence and Terrorism)?"

Similar Expressions:

▶ "Israelis need to protect themselves from Palestinian violence."

▶ "Hamas is a terrorist organization; Israel needs to defend itself from terrorism."

▶ "Israel needs to defend itself from the terrorists."

▶ "What do you expect Israel to do when Hamas keeps firing rockets into Israel?"

▶ "What would you do if Mexico sent rockets into the US?"

Related Facts:

• If *terrorism* is defined to be the threat or use of violence against civilians for economic or political purposes, then opposition—including violent opposition— against a military power (soldiers) is not terrorism.

• More than 70 percent of the people living in Gaza are refugees of land that is in Israel. International law recognizes their right to return to that land.

• In addition to those in Gaza, millions of Palestinians are internationally recognized legal refugees who have been blocked by the state of Israel from returning.

• Israeli laws are enforced against the people in the occupied Palestinian territories. Israel controls the Gaza population registry, its airspace, its access to imports and exports, and its territorial waters. <u>Gaza and West Bank residents require Israeli permits in order to leave</u> those territories.

- The notion of Mexico attacking us is not a good analogy for Gaza rockets into Israel. The United States does not occupy or blockade Mexico; most of the people in Mexico are not from North of the Rio Grande.

Unpacking the Israel Language:

The unspoken narratives underlying the question "Doesn't Israel have the right to defend itself (against Palestinian violence and terrorism)?" include the following:

▶ Israel is the victim rather than the oppressor.

▶ Israel is defending itself rather than attacking.

▶ A state, rather than its people, has rights.

▶ "Israel" does not include its indigenous people. Otherwise, how can a state defend itself from its own people?

▶ Israel has rights to the land it occupies.

The whole framing of Israel being defensive is important to put into context. We can skip over the everyday examples of oppression and attacks against Palestinians and still see the twisted framing of the Israel language. Just look at Israel's major historical milestones to deconstruct the Israelspeak:

- There is <u>nothing defensive</u> about Zionists having lobbied Great Britain in the early twentieth century, followed by the United States in the aftermath of World War II, for a Jewish state in Palestine against the wishes of the majority population.

- Evicting a majority of the indigenous population from the land in 1948 and not letting them return is not defensive; it is offensive.

- Taking land by force, even land beyond that allocated by the UN Partition Plan, which disproportionately favored Jews, is not defensive; it is offensive.

- Initiating the attacks on neighboring forces and taking land by force against international law, thereby more than doubling the size of Israel in the 1967 Six-Day War, is offensive rather than defensive.

- Occupying a population and violating their human rights for half a century is not defensive; it's offensive.

- Building settlements on occupied land against the Geneva Conventions is not defensive; it's offensive.

- Blockading a population of mostly children for over a decade and making Gaza unlivable according to the UN, are offensive and inhumane. Creating "the largest open-air prison" in the world, containing mostly children, is not defensive.

The Core Issues:

- Israel has always violated international law.
- Israel has always violated human rights.
- Israel has always been on the offense.

Recommended Approach and Sample Queries:

Your conversation with your partner works best if it is well planned and taken one step at a time. Where you are in your conversation and what you have covered before this question can affect your approach. If your conversation has made it clear that Israel is a racist state, then your answer to this question can be quick. Here is the query you can ask: "Do you believe a racist state, a state that has violated human rights since its founding, should be protected?"

If you have not yet reached clarity on Israel's racist nature, you will need to find out some basic information. Does your conversation partner consider the occupied Palestinian territories to be part of Israel? Most likely, they will consider East Jerusalem and maybe the West Bank—but maybe not Gaza—as part of Israel. Nonetheless, it helps to have them specify what "Israel" is. Ask, "What is Israel? What land does it include or not include?" If they respond, "The Jewish state," insist on their specifying the boundaries. You say, "Everyone has the right to defend himself or herself, except when that person is in my house and robbing me." Therefore, insist on knowing the context around the question they are asking you.

Now that you know what your conversation partner considers to be Israel, you need to find out who the "enemy" is. You might ask, "Can you tell me a situation and/or an enemy from which Israel needs to defend itself?" This will help identify the enemy. Most likely, they will tell you the Palestinians—most likely, the Palestinians in Gaza.

After identifying the enemy, your next step is to clarify what the "right to defend itself" against that enemy really means in Israel.

If your conversation partner tells you Hamas is the enemy, then ask them why all non-Hamas Palestinians are not granted citizenship. Your partner will likely oppose granting Israeli citizenship to all non-Hamas Palestinians, demonstrating that Hamas is not the real enemy.

If they tell you the enemy is Palestinians in Gaza, then ask them why they don't stand for letting those Palestinians return to their homelands; they would then be like Israeli Palestinians—no longer enemies. Again, Gaza is not the real enemy.

If they tell you it is because Palestinians (in Gaza, the West Bank, and in the diaspora) are not Israeli citizens, then ask them why those Palestinians don't have the same rights to citizenship as Jews.

The answer you are most likely to hear is that giving all Palestinians Israeli citizenship would mean the end of the Jewish state since Jews would no longer be a majority.

In the Israel language, *defensiveness* is maintaining a Jewish "majority," which unfortunately requires the violation of human rights of the true majority.

Here is a query you can pose to summarize: "When you ask me if Israel has the right to defend itself, aren't you really asking me if I will endorse Israel attacking people who want to exercise their international Right of Return and go home to their villages in Israel?" You can conclude with the following statement: "I am sorry, but I do not support a racist state violating human rights to maintain its ethnic identity."

Here are some additional queries you might use, depending on where you are in your conversation when the issue of Israel's "right to defend itself" comes up:

- **Right to self-defense:**
  - ❷ "Does a country or its people have the right to self-defense?"

  - ❷ "What does it mean for a state to defend itself from its people (or from the people it controls)?"

  - ❷ "What does it mean for a country to not recognize as its people a population that has always lived on the land that country controls?"

  - ❷ "When a country attacks the people it controls—the people whose human rights it violates—does that attack constitute *defense* or *oppression*?"

- **Who is "Israel"?**

  - ❷ "Is 'Israel' the people who have lived under the state of Israel's jurisdiction and control since that state took control of the land? Why not?"

  - ❷ "Is 'Israel' primarily people selected by ethnicity or religion (or people whose citizenship is granted or denied based on those criteria)?"

    - ❷ "If so, then does a racist or religiously discriminatory state have the right to 'defend itself' (especially from people it rules over who seek equality)?"

    - ❷ "If so, does an ethnic or religiously discriminatory state have the right to designate attacks against those whom it oppresses 'defense'? Did the Confederacy in the American Civil War have the right to 'defend itself' against revolting slaves?"

- **Israel's history of "self-defense":**

  - ❷ "Is aggression against the people Israel occupies and whose rights Israel has always violated 'defensive'?"

  - ❷ "Was it 'defensive' for Zionists to lobby superpowers to give them someone else's land?"

  - ❷ "Was it 'defensive' to violently take the land in 1948 and then ethnically cleanse the majority of the indigenous population from the land?"

  - ❷ "Is the blockade of Gaza 'defensive'?"

❷ "Is a blockade—particularly one of a population of whom 70 percent are refugees and more than 50 percent are children—'defensive'?"

❷ "What is 'defensive' about preventing medical supplies and food from getting into a territory? What is 'defensive' about preventing exports from leaving a territory?"

❷ "What is 'defensive' about occupying a population and denying them rights to citizenship, self-determination, and freedom of movement for more than fifty years?"

❷ "What is 'defensive' about destroying hundreds of thousands of homes and forcing the families out and then moving another population onto that land under armed guard?"

❷ "What is 'defensive' about systematically kidnapping children from their beds in their homes and interrogating them without legal or family representation and then pressing them to sign confessions in a language they don't understand?"

❷ "What is 'defensive' about blocking UN special rapporteurs and human rights organizations from observing the situation in the areas they cover?"

8. "Israel Has Always Had to Defend Itself from Aggressive Arab Nations."

Similar Expressions:

▶ "The War of Independence started when Arab neighbors attacked the newly formed state of Israel."

▶ "Iran wants to wipe Israel off the map!"

Related Facts:

- After no war has any Arab country controlled Israeli land.

- Arab armies attacked Israel only after May 15, 1948, after Zionists had spent six months ethnically cleansing hundreds of thousands of Palestinians from their homes. (See *How I Learned to Speak Israel* for the history).

- When Israel declared itself a state, it had already taken by force far more land than the UN had designated as part of the Jewish-majority state. (See *How I Learned to Speak Israel* for the history).

- Both the 1917 Balfour Declaration and the 1947 UN General Assembly Resolution 181, which approved the partitioning of Palestine into two states and the establishing of an international Jerusalem, stated that the Palestinians were not to be discriminated against in Israel/Palestine.

- Today, Israel controls land it took by force from all of its neighbors. It conquered Gaza from Egypt, Shebaa Farms from Lebanon/Syria, the Golan Heights from

Syria, and the West Bank (including East Jerusalem) from Jordan.

- Arab neighbors have been hosting millions of Palestinian refugees who are waiting to return to their homeland, but Israel has denied Palestinians their right to return.

- Israel initiated the 1967 Six-Day War, and it took only six days for it to more than double the land under its control.

- Egypt signed a peace treaty with Israel on March 26, 1979.[33]

- Jordan signed a peace treaty with Israel on October 26, 1994.[34]

- Iran is not Arab; it's mostly Persian. Iran is also not a neighbor.

Unpacking the Israel Language:

How much an unspoken narrative applies to you or resonates with you depends on your background. If you were raised in an anti-Arab environment (family, religious organization, school, etc.), then more of these unspoken narratives will ring true. The statement that Israel has had to defend itself from its Arab neighbors can generate the following unspoken narratives:

▸ The issue/conflict is about Arab countries, not about Palestinians.

▸ Israel is the innocent victim.

▸ Israel is not aggressive.

▸ Arab countries are the aggressors.

▸ Arabs don't want a Jewish state (and that is why they attacked immediately after Israel declared itself a state).

▸ Arab countries gang up on poor little Israel.

▸ Arabs hate Jews.

▸ Jews don't hate Arabs, but they need to defend themselves from Arabs.

▸ Iran is Arab.

Israel lobbied with the UK and the US to enable Zionists to take control of a land against the will of the land's population. Zionists took control of the land within the 1949 Armistice Demarcation Line (known as the Green Line), the land that is commonly recognized as the state of Israel, by force and expelled the majority of the non-Jewish population. Ethnic cleansing is offensive, not defensive. In the 1967 Six-Day War, Israel was the first to attack, catching its Arab neighbors by such a surprise that Egypt's air force was destroyed on the ground. More than doubling the size of the country in six days, as Israel did in 1967, is aggressive. Finally, holding a population under occupation for more than fifty years and under blockade for more than a decade is aggressive and inhumane.

Israel today occupies land it has taken by force from each of its neighbors: Gaza from Egypt, Shebaa Farms from Lebanon,[4] the Golan Heights from Syria, and the

---

4   There is a history of Shaba'a Farms being part of both Lebanon and Syria.

West Bank, including East Jerusalem, from Jordan. None of the Arab neighbors control land taken by force from Israel.

With this history as context, it is logical that Israel's neighbors would be aggressive towards Israel. Only ignorance of the history would make one believe that those who took the land by force are the victims. It is also understandable that people, and especially people of the region, would be opposed to a state that has sent them so many refugees.

The Core Issue:

Arab country aggression is rooted in Zionist aggression against Palestinians.

- Aggression from Arab countries is the result of direct Israeli aggression toward those countries or Israeli violation of Palestinian rights.

- Israel and the Zionist movement are the primary aggressors.

Recommended Approach and Sample Queries:

Be careful not to fall under the Israel language spell that "Israel has always had to defend itself from aggressive Arab nations"; don't get distracted from the real aggression. I translate this statement into English as follows: "Israel received military responses in 1948 from its Arab neighbors after it had expelled hundreds of thousands of Palestinians, destroyed hundreds of villages, and taken even more land than had been allocated to it by the UN Partition Plan. Israel also received a response after it attacked these countries in 1967, and since then the countries have tried to recapture lands that Israel took by force."

As is often the case on the subject of Israel, you need to find out how much your conversation partner knows. The first place to start would be to make sure they know the basic context. Start with questions such as:

❓ "Why are we talking about Arab countries when this is about Palestinian human rights?"

❓ "Do you know that the first time Arab armies attacked Israel or came into Palestine was after Zionist militias, which became Israeli forces, had forced out hundreds of thousands of Palestinians and that for up to six months, those refugees had been escaping the militias by fleeing into neighboring Arab countries?" (If your conversation partner is not aware of that fact, then recommend *The Birth of the Palestinian Refugee Problem Revisited* by Israeli historian Benny Morris.[35] It details which Palestinian village was emptied out on which date.)

❓ "Do you know that to this day, Israel has not allowed those Palestinians and their families to return?"

❓ "Are you aware that Israel was the first to attack in June 1967, catching the Arab militaries by surprise to the point of grounding the Egyptian air force?"

❷ "Are you aware that the land area Israel controlled more than doubled after only six days in the 1967 war?"

❷ "Are you aware that Israel controls land today that it took by force from each of its Arab neighbors, land that it was asked to return in UN Security Council Resolution 242?"

Then ask your conversation partner if they would again like to read their statement "Israel has always had to defend itself from aggressive Arab nations." If they are not embarrassed enough to retract their statement, you need to decide whether it is worth continuing a conversation with this person. The person would be like the burglar you tackle in your driveway after he has stolen your TV, complaining about his need to defend himself from your aggression.

If you genuinely believe your conversation partner is well-meaning and that queries might help them think about the issues, then here are three to consider:

❷ "How is it defensive to gain significant territory by force while attacking first?"

❷ "How is it defensive to take by force land from its neighbors?"

❷ "What is Israel defending if neighbors are coming to defend oppressed civilians?"

9. "The Security Fence/Wall/Barrier Is Needed to Protect Israel."

Similar Expressions:

▶ "The Security Fence protects Jews/Israelis from terrorism."

▶ "Terrorism has decreased because of the Security Fence."

Related Facts:

• The Security Fence (also known as the Apartheid Wall, or the Separation Barrier) is mostly inside the West Bank, not on the Green Line (the internationally recognized border between Israel and the occupied Palestinian territories). For simplicity we will call it the "barrier" in this chapter.

• More than 1.6 million Palestinians live on the Israeli side of the barrier, including those who are Israeli citizens and those who live in East Jerusalem.

Unpacking the Israel Language:

The following unspoken narratives can be derived from "The Security Fence/Wall/Barrier is needed to protect Israel":

▶ The barrier is on the border.

▶ The people on the other side of the barrier are a risk to Israel.

Most of the eighteen Israel expressions covered in this guide, and their respective unspoken narratives, are just false. By contrast, the statement "The Security Fence/Wall/Barrier is needed to protect Israel," and its unspoken narratives, contain grains of truth.

The grain of truth in the first unspoken narrative is that part of the barrier is on the internationally recognized border; the problem is that it is only a small percentage of the barrier that is on the border. The majority of the barrier is in the West Bank, carving up Palestinian territory. Initially, there were Palestinians on both sides, and the barrier limited their movement and their commerce. But systematically, Palestinian land on the "Israeli" side of the barrier has been, and continues to be, confiscated and bestowed on newer Jewish settler communities.

The grain of truth in the second unspoken narrative is more interesting because the people on the "other" side of the barrier are indeed a risk to Israel, not because they are a military or violence risk but because they are a demographic risk. The barrier has nothing to do with the risk; the Palestinians on both sides of the barrier are the demographic threat to Israel. If all the people in the occupied territories on both sides of the barrier were considered Israelis, then Israel would no longer be a Jewish state.

The Core Issue:

The barrier is not needed to protect Israel; violation of human rights is needed to protect Israel as a Jewish state. The barrier secures the violation of human rights.

The barrier is needed to force Palestinians into ghettos, to limit their ability to sustain themselves, and to ease confiscation of their land for Jews.

The barrier is a tool used to deny to Palestinians equality, citizenship, and the Right of Return.

Recommended Approach and Sample Queries:

"The Security Fence/Wall/Barrier is needed to protect Israel" is a well-disguised racist statement. I recommend that you respond to this statement by highlighting the lies and inhumanity of the Israeli enterprise. Show your conversation partner that for Israel, the word *security* in the statement really means supremacy, separation, and discrimination. And the phrase *to protect Israel* in the statement really means to consent to the transformation of an actual land theft into a constituted de facto situation, or as it is often called: a fact on the ground.

As mentioned elsewhere, first determine what your conversation partner already knows. Start by confirming some basic facts that are easily verifiable by both of you. You can ask the following queries:

❷ "Do you know that most of the barrier is in the West Bank and not on the Armistice Demarcation Line, also known as the 'Green Line'?"

❷ "Do you know that when the barrier was being built, it separated Palestinian neighborhoods from one another? For example, do you know that the wall separates Palestinians in East Jerusalem from Palestinians in the West Bank, both groups residing on land captured in 1967?"

❷ "Do you know that there are more than 1.6 million Palestinians on the 'Israeli' side of the barrier, including Palestinian Israeli citizens and East Jerusalemites?"

Once you have basic agreement on these facts, you can work with your conversation partner to establish what Israel is really up to:

❷ "Why is most of the barrier inside the West Bank rather than on the internationally recognized Green Line border?"

❷ "Why was the barrier built with Palestinians on both sides, separating families from their relatives and farmers from their land?"

❷ "If Palestinians are the 'security' threat, why has Israel subsidized moving hundreds of thousands of civilian Jews into the West Bank, and why are there more than 1.6 million Palestinians on the 'Israeli' side?"

❷ "Since the barrier is used to ethnically cleanse Palestinians from land they have lived on for centuries if not millennia, what does the word *security* really mean? Does it mean protection of the aggressor rather than the victim?"

GROUP 4:
Demonizing or Criticizing Palestinian Actions

Group 4 includes three Israel statements that demonize or criticize Palestinian actions:

10. **"Not all Palestinians are really refugees."**

11. **"Demanding Palestinians' Right of Return is a ploy to end the Jewish state."**

12. **"Palestinians and other Arabs are taught to hate Jews."**

Don't defend Palestinian crimes. Do focus on human rights. For example, civilians and occupied populations have the right to defend themselves against an outside military force. Don't let your conversation partner criticize Palestinians for asking for their Right of Return; the question is why does your conversation partner support a country that can't survive without violating that right.

10. "Not All Palestinians Are Really Refugees."

Similar Expressions:

▶ "Only the Palestinians who were forced to leave in 1948 are real refugees."

▶ "The UN treats Palestinians differently from others, in that descendants of expelled Palestinians are also counted as refugees, thereby inflating the number of refugees dramatically."

▶ "There are not millions of Palestinian refugees; there are fewer than fifty thousand still alive today."

▶ "Only the real refugees who were forced out should be allowed to return to Israel."

Related Facts:

• The UN does have an agency dealing specifically with Palestinians (the United Nations Relief and Works Agency for Palestine Refugees in the Near East, or UNRWA); however, both UNRWA and the United Nations High Commissioner for Refugees (UNHCR), the UN organization formed in 1950 for other refugees, recognize descendants as refugees.[36]

• As of August 2020, there are 5.6 million Palestinian refugees under UNRWA care.[37]

• Israel and Zionists claim that Jews have a right to "return" to Israel because their ancestors lived there thousands of years ago. Of course, none of those claiming that right today lived in Israel thousands of years ago. This is relevant because many Zionists claim that only those Palestinians who actually lived in Palestine in 1947 and who are still alive today might have a right to return. The racism is obvious: Zionists claim that Jewish descendants, but not Palestinian descendants, have a right to return.

Unpacking the Israel Language:

The statements "Not all Palestinians are really refugees" and "The UN treats Palestinians differently from others" contain the following unspoken narratives (as well as others):

- There *are* real Palestinian refugees!
▸ Palestinian refugees unfairly get special treatment, but they should be treated like other refugees.

First, it is very important that your conversation partner acknowledge that there are indeed Palestinian refugees. This acknowledgment opens up all kinds of questions as to why the refugees have not been allowed to return for more than seventy years. Why does your partner stand for a country that kills refugees who try to return (as in the Gaza Great March of Return)?

Second, it is the Jews, rather than the registered Palestinian refugees, who receive special treatment. Jews whose ancestors lost their German citizenship between 1933 and 1945 for political, racial, or religious reasons are welcomed by the German government and can receive German citizenship today.[38] By contrast, Palestinians are not permitted to reside or get citizenship in the land where they or their grandparents resided prior to 1948. Jews get the benefit of the Israeli "Law of Return" and can claim citizenship within forty-eight hours of arriving in Israel even if they can't name a single ancestor who ever lived in Israel. Palestinians, on the other hand, get "special treatment": They are denied their international Right of Return and are blocked from living in the house for which they still have the key or on the land to which they still hold a title. They cannot even gain citizenship in the land where their ancestors have lived for hundreds or thousands of years.

The Core Issue:

- It is Jews, not registered Palestinian refugees, who receive special treatment.

- Jews who have no ancestral claim to Israel can benefit from the Israeli "Law of Return" and can become citizens shortly after arrival there.

- By contrast, Palestinians with a proven ancestral claim to the land are denied their international Right of Return.

Recommended Approach (Sample Queries):

As usual, follow the theme of racism while trying to understand if and how your conversation partner has thought about these issues. Here are some queries:

❷ "You say that Palestinian refugees get special treatment. What treatment do Palestinian refugees get in Israel that Jews do not get? Are non-Israeli, nonrefugee Jews accorded any privileges that Palestinian refugees do not get?"

❷ "How can a country denying the Right of Return based on ethnicity not be racist?"

❷ "How is denying refugees their right to return based on ethnicity not ethnic cleansing?"

❷ "Does not this racist treatment sully the term *birthright*? Isn't *birthright* a racist term when applied to Israel?"

11. "Demanding Palestinians' Right of Return Is a Ploy to End the Jewish State."

Similar Expressions:

▶ "Allowing all Palestinians to return is a nonstarter."

▶ "Allowing Palestinian return is an existential threat to Israel."

▶ "Palestinian return threatens Israel's Jewish majority and is therefore not acceptable."

Related Fact:

• It is true that if a large number of Palestinian refugees returned to historic Palestine (now Israel, Gaza, and the West Bank) and were given equal rights, then there would be a Jewish minority in the land that Israel controls today.

Unpacking the Israel Language:

The statement "Demanding Palestinians' Right of Return is a ploy to end the Jewish state" is an acknowledgment of the fact that Israel requires the denial of human rights in order to exist as a Jewish-majority state.

The Core Issues:

• Why does your conversation partner support a state that requires the denial of human rights?

• Why does your partner stand for a racist state?

• Why is ethnic supremacy more important to your partner than human rights?

Recommended Approach (Sample Queries):

Ask any of the following queries you believe will be most effectively received:

❷ "Is your statement not an acknowledgment that the only way for Israel to exist as a Jewish-majority state is for it to violate human rights? If a state that violates human rights is not of concern, or if it is merely an unfortunate consequence of Israel's existence, then do you also accept other ethnically identified states, including those that violate Jewish human rights?"

❷ "Does it concern you that the only way for Israel to be a Jewish-majority state is for it to violate human rights?"

❷ "Isn't promoting a Jewish-majority state in historic Palestine itself a 'ploy' to deny human rights—maybe even in perpetuity? If so, does that concern you?"

12. "Palestinians and Other Arabs Are Taught to Hate Jews."

Similar Expressions:

▶ "Palestinians teach their children to hate Jews and Israel."

▶ "Hamas wants to wipe out Jews in Israel."

▶ "Israeli Jews need to protect themselves from these hateful Palestinians with a barrier and with occupation. Palestinians cannot be trusted."

Related Facts:

• There are more than 1.6 million Palestinian citizens of Israel. These are all on the Israeli side of any wall/fence/barrier, and they have the freedom to travel throughout Israel. Clashes are overwhelmingly between Jews and Palestinians in the occupied territories, where Palestinians do not have freedom or citizenship.

• Hamas kills fewer civilians (both in absolute number and in percentage) than does Israel.

• Israeli military service is required for Israeli Jews, and many are deployed to enforce the occupation and the denial of Palestinian human rights. Such violent racism would not be as easily implemented without the systematic differentiation and separation of Jews and Palestinians in Israeli schools and society.

• Approximately 40 percent of Israeli Jews believe that "Arabs" (that is, Israeli Palestinians) should have their right to vote for members in the Knesset revoked.[39] What makes that mentality possible?

Unpacking the Israel Language:

The unspoken narratives behind the statement "Palestinians and other Arabs are taught to hate Jews" include the following:

▶ Palestinian schoolbooks teach hatred toward Israel and Jews.

▶ Hate is evil, and because Palestinians teach hate, they are evil.

▶ Palestinians are the aggressors because they are filled with hate.

▶ Israel does not teach hatred of Arabs and Palestinians.

▶ Israel does not teach Palestinians to hate Israel and, by association, Jews.

Of course, each of these unspoken narratives creates a false paradigm. I do not want either side to teach hate or to be hateful. Israel is a very segregated society, and Arabs are portrayed as inferior in Israeli textbooks.[40] But if one wants to look at the most effective way to foster hate, then textbooks are only the beginning of the process.

The most effective tool for teaching hate, to both Jewish Israelis and Palestinians, is the occupation. The occupation requires Israel to teach Jews that Palestinians are their enemy and existential threat, and that Jews therefore need to hate Palestinians. If Israel did not teach Jews that Palestinians are different from them, that Palestinians are the enemy, then Israeli soldiers would not violate human rights and enforce the brutal occupation. If one wanted to teach Palestinians hate, there is no more effective way than the inhumane treatment by Israeli soldiers who violate human rights by enforcing the occupation and blockade.

The satirical site *The Onion* published an article during Israel's 2006 assault on Lebanon that facetiously explained the ill will toward Israel and, by association, toward Jews; it suggested that Israel was bombing anti-Semitism out of Lebanon.[41] You can use humor to show how ridiculous it is for someone to accuse the Arabs of teaching hatred when the Israeli occupation forces do a much better job by regularly entering Palestinian homes at night and taking children from their beds.[42]

The statement that Palestinians teach their children to hate is a Zionist projection of their own hatred for Palestinians. The evidence is clear. How could one convince teenagers to go into military service to violate people's human rights without first teaching them some sort of animosity toward the other people? How could one convince teenage soldiers to destroy people's homes and schools without first dehumanizing those people? The only way to convince young people to ethnically cleanse a land or bomb children is to demonize the other people. Why else would 40 percent of Israeli Jews believe that Israeli Palestinians should have their right to vote for members in the Knesset revoked?

In order to convince its population to violate Palestinians' human rights, Israel has to teach hate. If Israel cannot get its population to violate human rights, then it is no longer a Jewish-majority state. The evidence is clear: Palestinians want equality, whereas Israelis demand supremacy.

The Core Issues:

One does not occupy a people and violate human rights with love in one's heart.

Nothing teaches hatred better than abuse.

Recommended Approach and Sample Queries:

Direct the conversation to two primary points:

1. how hate is taught most effectively (by discrimination and violations of dignity)

2. who requires hatred in order to survive

Here are some sample queries to help you focus on those two points:

❷ "Do you believe that young Israelis could destroy people's homes, kidnap children from their beds in the middle of the night, torture people, demand that they disrobe at a checkpoint, and violate human rights in many other ways if they hadn't been taught to hate, or at least discriminate against, Palestinians?"

❷ "How do you explain the video of an Israeli soldier shouting with joy as he successfully filmed an Israeli sniper killing an innocent, unarmed Palestinian in Gaza? What does that say about what those soldiers had been taught?"

❷ Assuming that your conversation partner is against the Palestinians' Right of Return: "Stepping back, what does it say about your upbringing that you think it is not only OK but best to support the ethnic cleansing of a people from a land beginning in 1948 and continuing until the present?" If your partner brings up Native Americans, just respond that there is no law and no government that restricts any Native American from residing in any part of the United States.

❷ "Do you believe that Israel could enforce the occupation and continuous violation of human rights against Palestinians if it taught equality and respect for Palestinians as brothers and sisters? If it did not teach children that Palestinians are the enemy, how could Israelis justify denying Palestinians human rights, equality, citizenship, and the international Right of Return?"

If your conversation partner insists on talking about Palestinian hatred, then you can go with the following:

❷ "Yes, learning to hate in school can be powerful and destructive. However, what do you think is a more effective way to teach hatred of another people: learning it in school from your teacher or having a group do one or more of the following:[5]

❷ Kidnap your brother from his bed in the night, abuse him, keep him in detention for six months,

---

5   These actions have all occurred, and some occur regularly.

and then demand payment for his release?" (About seven hundred Palestinian children are taken from their families every year and judged in a military system with a 99-percent conviction rate.[43]) Make you and your people go through humiliating, time-consuming checkpoints to go anywhere?"

❷ Limit your ability to go to the beach or to visit relatives (as well as limit your relatives' ability to visit you)?"

❷ Demolish your home and require your parents pay for the demolition costs?"

❷ Block your parents' access to their farmland?"

❷ Uproot or burn your parents' olive trees?"

❷ Shoot a rubber-coated metal bullet or tear gas canister into your cousin's head?"[44]

GROUP 5:
Describing an Alternative Reality

Group 5 includes four Israel statements that describe an alternative reality:

13. **"There is no occupation; all of Jerusalem, Judea, and Samaria are part of Israel."**

14. **"Gaza is not under occupation; it is under Hamas control."**

15. **"Jerusalem is the capital of Israel."**

16. **"Israel just wants peace."**

Each of these statements is based on a worldview that there is no occupation, or that there is no blockade, or that there are no Palestinian people in parts of the occupied territories. Try to move away from these statements; each is a dangerous place full of rabbit holes with no exit, since you and your conversation partner don't agree on foundational "facts."

Once again, this guide is short; it covers the logical problems with the Zionist narrative and only basic facts. Determine which facts you both can agree on. If all you can both agree on is that Israel is a Jewish state, then at least you can ask what the term *Jewish* means in that context. You can then lead the conversation to how Israel is a racist state rather than one that follows the Jewish values of radical inclusion and equality.

13. "There Is No Occupation; All of Jerusalem, Judea, and Samaria[6] Are Part of Israel."

Similar Expressions:

▶ "How can there be an occupation when Jerusalem is part of Israel?"

▶ "How can there be an occupation when the West Bank and the Golan Heights are part of Israel?"

Related Facts:

- The international community, as represented by the UN General Assembly as well as the Security Council, does not recognize those territories as part of Israel or Jerusalem as Israel's capital.

- Israel does not recognize as citizens the people who have lived in those territories since before the territories were under Israeli control.

- Palestinians in the occupied West Bank live under Israeli military law.

Unpacking the Israel Language:

As I've mentioned previously, unspoken narratives can be different for different people; therefore, not all of them may resonate with you. Nonetheless, each will resonate with someone. Narratives on this subject include the following:

---

6   Israel calls the West Bank Judea and Samaria.

- It's Israel's land.

- Palestinians do not have a right to that land.

- Palestinians are trespassing on Israeli land in Judea and Samaria (the West Bank).

- Why are you bothering me about my land?

The concept of the West Bank belonging to Israel has significant and sinister repercussions. It creates a justification for ethnically cleansing the West Bank of Palestinians. It also is a rationale that Israel supporters have used to exempt Israel from having to abide by the Geneva Conventions; if there is no occupation, then the conventions don't apply.

Declaring that the West Bank is part of Israel is a distraction from examining Israel's human rights violations. In particular, Israel supporters claim that the land is part of Israel and that there is therefore no occupation and any mention of the Geneva Conventions is irrelevant. Israel supporters are in effect admitting that they are violating human rights with their claim that they don't need to abide by the Geneva Conventions because they are using the claim of inapplicability of the conventions as the excuse for allowing human rights violations. Their position also lacks integrity because if they really believed the territories were part of Israel they would be standing for all its people being citizens and the end of military law in the West Bank.

The Core Issue:

We know Israel is occupying the territories because it denies Israeli citizenship to its occupied inhabitants and rules them under Israeli military, rather than civilian, law.

Recommended Approach (Sample Queries):

The statement "There is no occupation; all of Jerusalem, Judea, and Samaria are part of Israel" is Israelspeak. You need to call out your conversation partner's racism with simple questions, such as the following:

❷ "If there is no occupation and those lands are part of Israel, then why aren't all the people of those lands Israeli citizens?" (Hold your partner to the fact that racism is the answer.)

❷ "If there is no occupation, then doesn't that mean you believe in the one-state solution, where everyone has equal rights?" (If your partner says no, then ask, "How can it all be a single state without equal rights for all? Are you endorsing a racist state?")

❷ "Why are people in those 'unoccupied' lands under military law rather than civilian law?"

14. "Gaza Is Not under Occupation; It Is under Hamas Control."

Similar Expressions:

▸ "Gaza is not under Israeli blockade."

▸ "Israel left Gaza in 2005."

▸ "Israel gave Gaza to the Palestinians in 2005."

Related Facts:

• The International Criminal Court ruled on November 3, 2014, that Gaza is under Israeli occupation: "Israel remains an occupying power in Gaza despite the 2005 disengagement. In general, this view is based on the scope and degree of control that Israel has retained over the territory of Gaza."[45]

• Israel controls the registry of the people in Gaza.

• Israel controls Gaza's Mediterranean Sea access and its airspace.

• Israel controls imports into and exports from Gaza.

• Gaza residents require Israeli approval to travel anywhere, even to neighboring Egypt.

Unpacking the Israel Language:

The unspoken narratives underlying the statement "Gaza is not under occupation; it is under Hamas control" include the following:

▸ The problems of Gaza are not Israel's fault.

▸ The problems of Gaza are Hamas's fault.

▸ Gaza is not under Israeli control.

▸ Gaza is not part of Israel.

Although Israel no longer has settlements in Gaza, its military controls parts of Gaza territory and all of its sea access and airspace. Israel controls people's movement and access to the outside world as well as commercial traffic in and out of the territory.

The Core Issue:

Gaza is under Israeli control, and the suffering in Gaza is because of Israel's stranglehold on imports and exports, and its bombing of homes, schools, hospitals, and infrastructure, including power, water, and sewer systems.

Recommended Approach (Sample Queries):

Just ask basic questions to pinpoint your conversation partner's Israelspeak:

❷ "If Israel is not occupying Gaza, then who is restricting people in Gaza from getting within hundreds of yards of the Israeli fence?"

❷ "If Israel is not occupying Gaza, then why do people in Gaza require Israeli permits in order to leave Gaza?"

❷ "If Israel is not occupying Gaza, then why are resident fishers restricted from using Gaza's territorial waters, and why does Israel confiscate boats attempting to approach Gaza?"

❓ "If Israel is not occupying Gaza, then why does Israel control Gazan imports and exports?"

15. "Jerusalem Is the Capital of Israel."

Similar Expressions:

▶ "All of Jerusalem is part of Israel."

▶ "How can part of Jerusalem be the capital of a Palestinian state when all of Jerusalem is Israel's capital?"

Related Facts:

- Per the 1947 UN Partition Plan, all of Jerusalem was to be an internationally administered jurisdiction and not part of either the Jewish state or the Arab state.

- West Jerusalem was completely ethnically cleansed of Palestinians in 1948 by Zionist forces.

- Israel captured East Jerusalem in 1967 in the Six-Day War.

- Palestinians who have always lived in Jerusalem do not get Israeli citizenship; instead, they get residency that is subject to rescission.

- Therefore, Palestinians who were born in, and whose families are from, the place that Israel calls its capital—including Palestinians who have lived in Jerusalem since before the state of Israel existed—are not Israeli citizens.

Unpacking the Israel Language:

The unspoken narratives underlying the statement "Jerusalem is the capital of Israel" include the following:

▶ All of Jerusalem is part of Israel.

▶ Jerusalem cannot be a Palestinian capital if there were to be a Palestinian state."

Not only does the statement "Jerusalem is the capital of Israel" demonstrate a complete disregard for international law, the 1947 UN Partition Plan, and the Green Line demarcating Israel from the occupied territories, but it also highlights Israel's racism: Whether a person born in Jerusalem and having lived there their entire life can be an Israeli citizen depends on the person's ethnicity or religion.

The Core Issue:

The notion that Jerusalem is the capital of Israel demonstrates Israel's disregard for international law, reflects its disregard for the 1947 UN Partition Plan, and highlights its racism against the indigenous population.

Recommended Approach and Sample Queries:

Don't get into an argument as to whether Jerusalem is the capital of Israel. If your conversation partner is a Zionist, they may take the perspective that the whole world is anti-Semitic and that is why other countries deny the city to Israel. That conversation is unproductive.

It's far better to focus on the core of the Israel problem: It is founded on racism, and it requires racism to survive. Therefore, ask the questions that make it clear to your conversation partner that you know that they are making a conscious choice to support racism. Let them feel the heat.

Focus on fundamental questions whose answer is racism:

❷ "If Jerusalem is the capital of Israel, then why aren't all its people citizens of Israel?"

❷ "If Israel is a democracy, why don't all Jerusalemites have representation in the Knesset?"

16. "Israel Just Wants Peace."

Similar Expressions:

▸ "Israel has made numerous peace offers, which Palestinians have only rejected."

▸ "Israel offers peace, and Palestinians respond with terrorism."

▸ "Israel wants to negotiate for peace, but the Palestinians won't even come to the table."

▸ "Palestinians have never been a partner interested in peace."

▸ "Palestinians never miss an opportunity to miss an opportunity for peace."

▸ "As long as the Palestinian government is corrupt and divided, how can there be peace?"

Related Facts:

• Israel has never offered equal rights for Palestinians. Israel has claimed in the past to have given equal rights to Palestinian citizens of Israel; however, there are many Israeli laws that are discriminatory. More importantly, Israel has never given noncitizen Palestinians the same rights as noncitizen Jews—especially the right to citizenship.

• No Israeli offer has included the upholding of international law, including the Right of Return of refugees and equality for all people.

• Israel continues to put settlements in the West Bank and East Jerusalem while it demolishes Palestinian homes in Israel, East Jerusalem, the West Bank, and Gaza.

- Israel has never extended to Palestinians sovereignty over their land. For example, none of the so-called peace offers included the ability for Palestinians to have full control over their land, their airspace, their water rights, or their borders with other countries. All of the offers have stipulated that Israel retains some control.

- Israel has held Palestinians under military occupation for more than fifty years.

- No negotiations with Palestinians are necessary to bring equality to Israel/Palestine; Israel can make that move unilaterally.

- There is no real Palestinian government; what "Palestinian government" there is (the Palestinian National Authority, or PA) serves at the pleasure of the Israeli government. Israel has made a farce of democracy and the PA elections by detaining a number of Hamas officials shortly after they were elected in 2006. The PA enforces the occupation on behalf of and with Israel. Subsequently, Palestinians don't have much confidence in elections, as can be shown by the fact that Palestinian President Mahmoud Abbas has still not completed his four-year term from the election of 2005. A large proportion of the tax revenue in the PA budget is actually collected by Israel and then transferred to the PA, but Israel has suspended the transfers on a number of occasions.

Unpacking the Israel Language:

The statements "Israel just wants peace" and "Palestinians have never been a partner interested in peace" contain within them the following unspoken narratives:

▸ Israel is the peace-loving example.

▸ Palestinians are the violent and inhumane belligerents.

▸ Israel has extended reasonable offers to the Palestinians.

▸ The Palestinians have rejected reasonable Israeli offers.

▸ Israel's actions reflect its intent to be at peace with the Palestinians.

▸ Israel is not violent; Palestinians are violent.

▸ Israel and Palestine are equivalent, autonomous governments.

It is blatant Israelspeak to claim that Israel just wants peace when it has brutally occupied a civilian population for more than half a century; blockaded a predominantly child population in Gaza for more than a decade, making it unlivable as of 2020, according to the UN[46]; and violated the human rights of all Palestinians every day of Israel's existence.

There is nothing peaceful about the ethnic cleansing of the land, the demolishing of homes and schools, and the building of Jewish-only settlements on Palestinian land. If your conversation partner counters that the land is not Palestinian (even though it is considered Palestinian under international law), then ask, "Why have there been Palestinians on the land for five thousand years?"[47]

Israel's definition of *peace* entails the removal of Palestinians. Israel has never wanted peace with equality and justice, because that would be an existential threat to a Jewish state: As soon as Palestinians have equal rights, they are a majority.

Anyone making the statement "Israel just wants peace" either is ignorant about both the history and the present situation or defines *peace* to be forcing a population into submission and dispossession. From Albert Einstein to Martin Luther King Jr., and within numerous peace organizations, *peace* is defined not only as the absence of violence, tension, and war but also as the long-term presence of social justice and equality. Israel has never offered Palestinians the same rights as Jews, especially rights to citizenship or self-determination—hence, Israel has never offered Palestinians peace.

The Core Issue:

For Israel, peace entails the removal of Palestinians — ethnically cleansing the land by submission.

Real peace, with equality and justice across the land, has never been an interest for Israel because such peace is an existential threat to a Jewish-majority state.

Recommended Approach:

Again, focus on racism—but this time through the *peace* lens. Determine whether your conversational partner has ever thought about what *peace* requires. Does their *peace* require equality? Does their *peace* require justice? If not, what does their *peace* look like? Was there *peace* in the South before the American Civil War? Does your conversation partner think that slaves thought there was peace at that time? Does your partner think that ethnic supremacy can coexist with peace?

This conversation can go in many directions. Keep trying to understand how much your partner might have thought about the consequences of their position and how much or little they support racist ways.

Sample Queries to Learn from Your Conversation Partner:

❷ "What do you mean by *peace*?"

  ❷ "What do you think of MLK's statement 'True peace is not just the absence of tension; it is the presence of justice'?"

  ❷ "Do you believe that peace is possible without justice? Is justice possible without equality?"

❷ "Are human rights a requirement for peace? Are human rights negotiable? If so, then are they no longer rights?"

❷ "Can you describe what living in peace without human rights looks like? Is that what you support?"

❷ "When did Israel offer as part of any peace proposal equal rights for all Palestinians, including the right to citizenship for those in the diaspora?"

❷ "How does the occupation and blockade promote peace?"

❷ "If Israel wants peace, then why is it building Jewish-only settlements on Palestinian land? How does that help the peace process?"

❷ "How do home and school demolitions in the West Bank and Gaza demonstrate Israel's dedication to peace?"

❷ "If terrorism is the threat or use of violence against civilians for political or economic purposes, then is the occupation terrorism or peaceful?"

❷ "How is the continuous and systematic ethnic cleansing of Palestinians from 1948 until today an expression of Israel's wanting peace?"

GROUP 6:
Claiming That Israel Is Like the United States

Group 6 includes two Israel statements that claim that Israel is like the United States (that Americans should stand with Israel because Israel reflects Western and democratic values):

17. **"We should support the only democracy in the Middle East."**

18. **"We need to support Israel. They are like us; they have Judeo-Christian values."**

You may want to agree that both Israel and the United States have a history of racist settler colonialism. You can check whether your conversation partner thinks that Americans have a racism problem. You may want to share that at least in the US, we had a civil rights movement in the 1960s. You can ask if your partner believes that Israel will ever have equal rights for all.

17. "We Should Support the Only Democracy in the Middle East."

Similar Expression:

▶ "Israel is the only democracy in the Middle East."

Related Facts:

- Israel is not a real representative democracy, since it does not let all the governed vote for their government.

- Israel prevents democracy by restricting citizenship. For example, if one is born Palestinian in the city that Israel calls its capital, one does not get citizenship, even if one's family was there since before Israel controlled Jerusalem.

- Israel also is anti-democratic. Israel blocks Palestinians from self-determination—for example, it blocks statehood for Palestine in the UN, it arrests Palestinian Legislative Council elected officials, and it limits voting from Jerusalem.

- The Palestinian Authority is a democracy (when Israel lets it be one), and it is in the Middle East. There are other democratic forms of government in the Middle East, but like the United States, they are imperfect constitutional republics (Iran, Iraq, Lebanon, Turkey).

Unpacking the Israel Language:

The unspoken narratives underlying the statement "We should support the only democracy in the Middle East" include the following:

▶ Israel is a democracy.

▶ There are no other democracies in the Middle East.

▶ Israel is the country most like the US in the Middle East.

The Core Issue:

How can one call Israel a real democracy and a Jewish state when most of the people it governs are not Jewish?

If Israel were really a democracy, the majority would call it "Palestine."

Recommended Approach (Sample Queries):

Focus on the racism:

❓ "Is a country that bases citizenship on ethnicity a democracy?"

❓ "Can we legitimately call a long-term occupier that denies citizenship to those it governs a democracy?"

❓ "Can you explain what a 'Jewish democracy' means, especially when the majority of the population governed by Israel is not Jewish?"

18. "We Need to Support Israel. They Are Like Us; They Have Judeo-Christian Values."

Similar Expressions:

▸ "Israel is the only free economy in the Middle East."

▸ "Israel is the only country in the Middle East with Western values."

▸ "Israel is the only free society in the Middle East with respect for human rights."

Related Facts:

- Israel does not have a free economy; Palestinian businesses in the West Bank and Gaza are restricted.

- All countries in the Middle East are based on the Abrahamic faiths. The Abrahamic values are shared by Jews, Christians, and Muslims alike, and the Old Testament is foundational to all three faiths. Parts of so-called sharia law that Westerners object to, such as stoning someone to death, derive from the Bible. And is stoning much worse than solitary confinement followed by capital punishment in the US?

- Israel has always violated human rights (and it needs to do so in order to maintain a Jewish majority).

Unpacking the Israel Language:

The following are some of the unspoken narratives that underlie the statement "We need to support Israel" because "they are like us" in that "they have Judeo-Christian values":

▶ Israel is an oasis of civilization in a backward region of Muslim Arabs.

▶ Other countries in the region are Muslim and are therefore bad. (Whatever "bad" is.)

▶ Other countries in the region don't have Judeo-Christian values.

▶ Israel has values. Other countries in the region do not.

▶ We need to protect Israel from these barbarians.

The only reason to state that Israel is most like us and has Judeo-Christian values is to create an "us versus them" mindset. This statement puts Israel in the "us" camp and all other countries in the region in the "them" camp. The statement's wording plants the seed for at least discrimination if not outright hatred—which, ironically, is not a Judeo-Christian value. It is also ironic that these narratives overlook the fact that Islam is founded on Abrahamic values (comparable to the Judeo-Christian ones).

The Core Issues:

- Israel does not abide by Judeo-Christian values, and often we don't either.

- The cardinal Judeo-Christian value is to love your neighbor as yourself. A Jewish state is counter to that value.

- Creating an "us versus them" mindset is doing the opposite of loving our neighbor.

- Israel is founded on racism and requires racism to maintain its identity as a single-ethnic or a single-religious state.

- Racism is not a Jewish, a Christian, or a Muslim value.

Recommended Approach (Sample Queries):

Call out the sullying of Judeo-Christian values with questions like:

❓ "What does it say about us that we consider a country that is based on ethnic supremacy most like us?"

❓ "Since racism is required for Israel to survive, are you saying that racism is a Judeo-Christian value?"

Now What?

Now that you have read a number of these Israel expressions (questions and statements) and their corresponding response queries, you may be wondering how all of us got into this mess. How is it that so many American Jews and American Christians—in fact, so many Americans in general—have come around to stand behind a state that violates our foundational values? As you struggled with some of these queries, you probably observed how they highlight the illogical nature of what you may have been taught and told. This pulling the rug out from under your understanding may make you wish you had more background on the issue—not just queries but also some answers. Maybe you would like more knowledge to build your confidence as you think about and ask these queries.

My turning point occurred when I heard something on the news that conflicted with what I had been taught; it made me question what I had understood about the situation. I started researching and asking more questions, embarking on a journey of discovery about history, politics, and messaging. That journey has provided the base from which I can comfortably ask these queries to conversation partners today.

I welcome you on this journey with me. By reading my book *How I Learned to Speak Israel*, you can develop that comfort and build that confidence with a growing knowledge of history, politics, and language. (You can get the book at HowToSpeakIsrael.com.)

You can also learn a lot on your own, as I did. Some great places to broaden your learning include, among many more, the following:

- **International organizations:**
  - United Nations Relief and Works Agency for Palestine Refugees in the Near East (UNRWA.org)
- **Israeli organizations:**
  - *B'Tselem*, the Israeli Information Center for Human Rights in the Occupied Territories (BTselem.org)
  - ICAHD-USA, the Israeli Committee against House Demolitions–USA (ICAHDUSA.org)
  - MachsomWatch, Women for Human Rights and against the Occupation (MachsomWatch.org/en)
  - Breaking the Silence (BreakingTheSilence.org.il)
- **Jewish organizations in the US:**
  - Jewish Voice for Peace (JVP.org)
  - If Not Now (IfNotNowMovement.org)
  - Center for Jewish Nonviolence (CJNV.org)
- **Palestinian organizations:**
  - Al-Haq, a Palestinian human rights organization based in Ramallah, West Bank. (AlHaq.org)

- BADIL Resource Center for Palestinian Residency and Refugee Rights, an independent, human rights non-profit organization. (BADIL. org/en)

- Defense for Children International – Palestine, a Palestinian human rights organization focused on child rights. (DCI-Palestine.org)

- Palestinian BDS National Committee (BNC), a coalition of Palestinian organizations (BDSMovement.net)

- Palestinian Centre for Human Rights, a Palestinian human rights organization based in Gaza City. (PCHRGaza.org/en)

- **Palestinian support organizations:**

  - US Boats to Gaza, a partner of the International Freedom Flotilla Coalition (USBoatsToGaza.org)

  - If Americans Knew (IfAmericansKnew.org)

  - US Campaign for Palestinian Rights (USCPR.org)

- **US and international peace and human rights organizations:**

  - CODEPINK (CodePink.org)

  - The "No Way to Treat a Child" campaign of Defense for Children International–Palestine and American Friends Service Committee (NoWayToTreatAChild.org)

  - Amnesty International (Amnesty.org)

  - Human Rights Watch (HRW.org)

- **Religious organizations:**

  - Kairos Palestine (KairosPalestine.ps)

  - Friends of Sabeel North America: A Christian Voice for Palestine (FOSNA.org)

  - American Friends Service Committee (AFSC.org)

  - American Muslims for Palestine (AMPalestine.org)

  - True Torah Jews (TrueTorahJews.org)

APPENDIX:
Why Call It
When They Speak Israel?

A number of people have asked me why I use the term *Speak Israel*. The phrase particularly bothers English professionals who point out that it is grammatically incorrect; for example, one does not say, "Speak England." It may bother others because people may not be consciously "speaking Israel." In response to these very reasonable questions and concerns, I thought it would be appropriate to explain my reasoning for the title.

One aspect of the Israel language is that it is hard to distinguish (from English). If one is not analyzing statements and questions with the context of Israel's occupation or history in mind, it is easy to miss the fact that an expression is in Israel rather than in English. Similarly, if you see the word *Israel* in a sentence and you are not considering the context, you may think it is referring to the country or a people. One needs to be on one's toes, paying close attention, to identify Israel language. If I had named the language "Israeli" or "Israelish" or "Israelese," one would miss Israel's sneakiness. If it were clear, it would not be speaking Israel.

Unlike other languages, which are intended to help people communicate, Israel is a language that is intended to deceive. Therefore, I didn't want it to sound like other languages that end in *-ish* or *-ese*.

Another reason for choosing the *Speak Israel* expression is that something seems wrong when reading those two words. Something seems odd with *Speak Israel*. So it is when one is reading or hearing the Israel language. Is it not odd for someone to be accused of anti-Semitism, a form of racism, when they are standing for equality? That is why I wrote this guide, to help you figure out what is wrong with the Israel statements and questions: *When They Speak Israel* points you to the deception.

Finally, the best reason for naming the language "Israel" is that the language's only purpose is to promote the state of Israel. The Israel language is successful when it convinces people that a racist country is moral or when it prevents people from speaking out against the state's crimes.

I felt that George Bernard Shaw's quote was appropriate as this book's epigraph for three reasons. First, "the single biggest problem in communication is the illusion that it has taken place" seemed appropriate because I wrote this book in response to my frustration in not being able to communicate. Second, I wanted to make sure that I was communicating as clearly as possible because the Israel language is hard to detect; it is camouflaged as English, and precise and clear instruction is therefore needed to identify its use. And finally, I thought Shaw's quote was appropriate because it can also be an Israel expression. Yes, Israel was spoken before you got to the table of contents. Referring to the Israel language and translating the quote from Israel into English, one gets: "The single biggest problem in (Israel) communication is that the illusion has taken place."

Endnotes

1. *Merriam-Webster Dictionary*, s.v. "ethnic," accessed August 17, 2020, https://www.merriam-webster.com/dictionary/ethnic.

2. *Merriam-Webster Dictionary*, s.v. "race," accessed August 17, 2020, https://web.archive.org/web/20190121202725/https://www.merriam-webster.com/dictionary/race

3. UN General Assembly, Resolution 2106 (XX), International Convention on the Elimination of All Forms of Racial Discrimination (December 21, 1965, in force January 4, 1969), accessed August 12, 2020, https://www.ohchr.org/EN/ProfessionalInterest/Pages/CERD.aspx.

4. Agence France-Presse, "Benjamin Netanyahu Says Israel Is 'Not a State of All Its Citizens,'" *The Guardian*, March 10, 2019, accessed September 22, 2019, https://www.theguardian.com/world/2019/mar/10/benjamin-netanyahu-says-israel-is-not-a-state-of-all-its-citizens.

5. "Munayyer and Beinart's Historic Debate on the Solution to the Conflict," *Arab America*, June 6, 2015, accessed August 12, 2020, https://www.arabamerica.com/munayyer-and-beinarts-historic-debate-on-the-solution-to-the-conflict/.

6. *Merriam-Webster Dictionary*, s.v. "anti-Semitic," accessed August 5, 2020, https://www.merriam-webster.com/dictionary/anti-Semitic.

7. International Holocaust Remembrance Alliance, "Working definition of Antisemitism," accessed August 5, 2020, https://www.holocaustremembrance.com/working-definition-antisemitism.

8. Kenneth Stern, "I Drafted the Definition of Antisemitism. Rightwing Jews Are Weaponizing It," *The Guardian*, December 13, 2019, accessed January 11, 2021, https://www.theguardian.com/commentisfree/2019/dec/13/antisemitism-executive-order-trump-chilling-effect.

9. *Merriam-Webster Dictionary*, s.v. "Semite," accessed August 5, 2020, https://www.merriam-webster.com/dictionary/Semite.

10. Barbara Bibbo, "Israel Gets Flak over Human Rights Record in Geneva," Al-Jazeera Media Network, January 24, 2018, accessed October 21, 2020, https://www.aljazeera.com/news/2018/01/israel-flak-human-rights-record-geneva-180123180839181.html.

11. "Israel Expels Human Rights Watch Director Today: Group Will Keep Documenting Abuses by All Parties," Human Rights Watch, November 25, 2019, accessed November 30, 2019, https://www.hrw.org/news/2019/11/25/israel-expels-human-rights-watch-director-today.

12. "No Way to Treat a Child," American Friends Service Committee, September 10, 2015, accessed August 28, 2020, https://www.afsc.org/story/no-way-to-treat-child.

13. "Factsheet: Palestinian Children in the Israeli Military Detention System," No Way to Treat a Child, Defense for Children International–Palestine, March 5, 2020, accessed August 6, 2020, https://nwttac.dci-palestine.org/factsheet_military_detention.

14. Imogen Foulkes, "Global Refugee Figures Highest Since WW2, UN Says," BBC News, last modified June 20, 2014, accessed March 3, 2020, https://www.bbc.com/news/world-27921938; "Palestine Refugees: Locations and Numbers," Migration, *New Humanitarian*, last modified January 16, 2010, accessed March 3, 2020, http://www.thenewhumanitarian.org/report/89571/middle-east-palestinian-refugee-numberswhereabouts

15. Adam Withnall, "Amnesty International Reveals the 10 Worst Attacks on Human Rights across the World Last Year," *The Independent*, February 24, 2016, accessed August 12, 2020, https://www.independent.co.uk/news/world/politics/amnesty-international-reveals-the-10-worst-attacks-on-human-rights-across-the-world-last-year-a6892911.html

16. "US Foreign Aid by Country" (Israel, 2018, Obligations, All Agencies), USAID Foreign Aid Explorer, accessed August 5, 2020, https://explorer.usaid.gov/cd/ISR?fiscal_year=2018&measure=Obligations

17. "Leahy Fact Sheet," US Department of State, March 9, 2018, accessed August 6, 2020, https://www.state.gov/leahy-fact-sheet/.

18. Donald Neff, "An Updated List of Vetoes Cast by the United States to Shield Israel from Criticism by the U.N. Security Council," *Washington Report on Middle East Affairs*, May–June 2005, 14 [updated January 10, 2017], accessed October 12, 2020, https://www.wrmea.org/005-may-june/an-updated-list-of-vetoes-cast-by-the-united-states-to-shield-israel-from-criticism-by-the-u.n.-security-council.html

19. Withnall, "Amnesty International Reveals the 10 Worst Attacks on Human Rights across the World Last Year."

20. "Each Year the Israeli Military Detains and Prosecutes Around 700 Palestinian Children," No Way to Treat a Child," Defense for Children

International–Palestine and American Friends Service Committee, accessed August 5, 2020, https://nwttac.dci-palestine.org/.

21. "Global Trends: Forced Displacement in 2019," UN High Commissioner for Refugees (UNHCR), accessed August 5, 2020, https://www.unhcr.org/globaltrends2019/

22. "The Balfour Declaration," In Depth: Israel and the Palestinians: Key Documents, BBC News, November 29, 2001, accessed October 16, 2020, http://news.bbc.co.uk/2/hi/in_depth/middle_east/israel_and_the_palestinians/key_documents/1682961.stm

23. UN General Assembly, Resolution 181 (II), Future Government of Palestine (November 29, 1947), accessed September 29, 2020, https://unispal.un.org/UNISPAL.NSF/5ba47a5c6cef541b802563e000493b8c/7f0af2bd-897689b785256c330061d253?OpenDocument

24. "The Balfour Declaration," In Depth: Israel and the Palestinians: Key Documents.

25. UN Special Committee on Palestine (UNSCOP), "Question of Palestine/ Partition Recommendation," Report Addendum 1 (Annexes, Appendix and Maps), April 1947, accessed October 16, 2020, https://www.un.org/unispal/document/auto-insert-186346/

26. UN General Assembly, Resolution 181 (II), Future Government of Palestine (November 29, 1947).

27. Kashira Gander, "Vatican Recognises Palestine as State in Treaty," Independent, May 13, 2015, accessed October 16, 2020, https://www.independent.co.uk/news/world/politics/vatican-recognises-palestine-state-treaty-10248198.html

28. Steven Sellers Lapham, "Ten U.S. Churches Now Sanction Israel— To Some Degree, and with Caveats," *Washington Report on Middle East Affairs*, March–April 2019, 51–53, accessed October 19, 2020, https://www.wrmea.org/2019-march-april/ten-us-churches-now-sanction-israel-to-some-degree-and-with-caveats.html

29. Josh. 23:15–16 (New International Version).

30. Judg. 2:20–23 (NIV).

31. Matt. 7:12 (NIV).

32. Matt. 7:15–16 (NIV).

33. "Israel-Egypt Peace Treaty," Israel Ministry of Foreign Affairs, March 26, 1979, accessed August 28, 2020, https://mfa.gov.il/mfa/foreignpolicy/peace/guide/pages/israel-egypt%20peace%20treaty.aspx

34. "Israel-Jordan Peace Treaty," Israel Ministry of Foreign Affairs, October 26, 1994, accessed August 28, 2020, https://mfa.gov.il/mfa/foreignpolicy/peace/guide/pages/israel-jordan%20peace%20treaty.aspx

35. Benny Morris, The Birth of the Palestinian Refugee Problem Revisited (Cambridge, UK: Cambridge University Press, 2004).

36. "Convention and Protocol Relating to the Status of Refugees," UN High Commissioner for Refugees (UNHCR), accessed August 13, 2020, https://www.unhcr.org/en-us/3b66c2aa10

37. United Nations Relief and Works Agency for Palestine Refugees in the Near East (UNRWA), accessed August 12, 2020, https://www.unrwa.org/

38. "Illegitimate Children of Jews Evicted by Nazis Are German Citizens, Court Rules," *Reuters World News*, June 17, 2020, accessed October 20, 2020, https://www.reuters.com/article/us-germany-nazi-citizenship-idUSKBN23O1O6

39. Roee Nahmias, "'Marriage to an Arab Is National Treason,'" *Ynet News*, March 27, 2007, accessed September 2, 2019, https://www.ynetnews.com/articles/0,7340,L-3381978,00.html

40. Nurit Peled-Elhanan, *Palestine in Israeli School Books: Ideology and Propaganda in Education* (London: I.B. Tauris, 2012).

41. "Israel Bombs Anti-Semitism Out of Lebanon," *The Onion*, December 18, 2006, accessed October 3, 2020, https://www.theonion.com/israel-bombs-anti-semitism-out-of-lebanon-1819568873

42. "No Way to Treat a Child."

43. "Struggle of Palestinians Directed at Colonial Occupation of Land, People, Not Judaism, Permanent Observer Tells Solidarity Meeting: Secretary-General Calls for Talks to Support Intra-Palestinian Reconciliation," UN General Assembly, Committee on the Inalienable Rights of the Palestinian People (UN Meetings Coverage and Press Releases), November 28, 2018, accessed October 16, 2020, https://www.un.org/press/en/2018/gapal1418.doc.htm

44. "The Story behind Ahed Tamimi's Slap: Her Cousin's Head Shattered by Israeli Soldier's Bullet," *Israel-Palestine News* (If Americans Knew), January 4, 2018, accessed August 28, 2020, https://israelpalestinenews.org/story-behind-ahed-tamimis-slap-cousins-head-shattered-israeli-soldiers-bullet/

45. "Situation on Registered Vessels of Comoros, Greece and Cambodia: Article 53(1) Report," Office of the Prosecutor, International Criminal Court, Introduction, item 27, November 6, 2014, accessed February

22, 2018, http://opiniojuris.org/wp-content/uploads/2014-11-03-Final-Report-on-Situation-ICC-01.13.pdf

46. "Gaza 'Unliveable,' UN Special Rapporteur for the Situation of Human Rights in the OPT Tells Third Committee (Press Release Excerpts)," United Nations, "The Question of Palestine," 73rd Session, 31st and 32nd Meetings, October 24, 2018, accessed October 4, 2020, https://www.un.org/unispal/document/gaza-unliveable-un-special-rapporteur-for-the-situation-of-human-rights-in-the-opt-tells-third-committee-press-release-excerpts/

47. Marc Haber, Claude Doumet-Serhal, Christiana Scheib, et al., "Continuity and Admixture in the Last Five Millennia of Levantine History from Ancient Canaanite and Present-Day Lebanese Genome Sequences," *American Journal of Human Genetics (AJHG)* 101, no. 2 (August 3, 2017): 274–282, accessed October 21, 2020, https://www.cell.com/ajhg/fulltext/S0002-9297(17)30276-8

9 781954 221017